BUILDING BRIDGES

Community and University Partnership in East St. Louis

Kenneth M. Reardon

For permission requests, write to the publisher below:
Social Policy Press
2221 St. Claude Avenue, New Orleans, LA 70117 (physical)
PO Box 3924, New Orleans, LA 70177 (mailing)
Tel: (504) 302-1238 | www.socialpolicypress.org

Ordering information

Quantity sales
Special discounts are available on quantity purchases by corporations,
associations and others. For details, contact the Publisher at the Social Policy
address above.

Individual sales
Social Policy Press publications are available through bookstores. They can also
be ordered directly from Social Policy Press at the above numbers and through
socialpolicy.org.

Orders for college textbook/course adoption use
Contact Social Policy Press (504) 302-1238

Orders for U.S. and other trade bookstores and wholesalers
Please contact Social Policy Press or visit our website's

Social Policy Press is a registered trademark of
Labor Neighbor Research and Training Center, Inc.

Printed in the United States of America.

Reardon, Kenneth M.
Building Bridges: Community and University Partnerships in East St. Louis
ISBN 978-0-9970943-5-0
1. Community development
2. Local and regional planning
3. University projects and partnerships

First edition
Layout and design: Hatty Lee Lin, Sunnyvale, California
Copyediting: Mary Rowles, Salt Spring, British Columbia and
Wade Rathke, New Orleans
Index: Marie Hurt, New Orleans

With deep gratitude to my wife, Kathy, whose unwavering commitment to social justice both inspired and supported the work described in this book.

TABLE OF CONTENTS

TABLE OF ILLUSTRATIONS

INTRODUCTION

THIS BOOK CHRONICLES the efforts that residents from one of America's poorest cities and their university allies made to improve the quality of life in East St. Louis at a time when few urban scholars and policy-makers believed so-called Legacy Cities, such as: East St. Louis, Illinois; Providence, Rhode Island; Bridgeport, Connecticut; Buffalo, New York; Camden, New Jersey; Wilkes-Barre, Pennsylvania; Youngstown, Ohio; Detroit, Michigan; St. Louis, Missouri; and Memphis, Tennessee could be successfully redeveloped. The book describes how residents of East St. Louis' Emerson Park, Lansdowne, Olivette Park, Winstanley/ Industry Park, Edgemont, Alta Sita and the South End neighborhoods collaborated with University of Illinois Urbana-Champaign (UIUC) students to design and implement projects aimed at stabilizing and ultimately revitalizing their neighborhoods.

Undeterred by the pessimism of mainstream academic discourse and the cynicism of contemporary political debates, these residents and their university partners, mobilized dozens of local institutions and thousands of community stakeholders and university students between 1990 and 2000 to successfully implement an impressive series of community development projects that helped stabilize several of the city's most distressed neighborhoods. Along the way, these leaders devised a highly participatory approach to community development, referred to as empowerment planning, that integrated the central principles and techniques of participatory action research, direct action organizing, and popular education into a highly effective community transformation process that was successfully applied throughout East St. Louis and subsequently replicated in several other economically challenged cities in the U.S. and abroad. The primary goal of this approach to planning is to enhance the capacity of resident-led development organizations in economically distressed communities to influence the public and private investment decisions that, to a large degree, determine the quality of urban and rural life.

This book describes how a small group of neighborhood residents angered by East St. Louis' ongoing economic collapse and physical deterioration supported by university students and faculty overcame significant geographic distance and racial, class, religious, age, and gender differences to stabilize the poorest neighborhoods in a failing industrial city located in the American heartland. It is an uplifting story of the faith, courage, and creativity of East St. Louis' grassroots leaders and their university allies that reminds us of the enduring truth of Margaret Meade's statement, "Never doubt that a small group of thoughtful, committed citizens can change the world. Indeed, it's the only thing that ever has." The residents, students, and faculty who participated in this effort hope the lessons learned outlined in the last chapter of this book can assist those currently working in similarly challenging circumstances.

The Urban Extension and Minority Access Project, which began with a single urban design studio in 1987 evolved, over time, into a campus-wide outreach effort that came to symbolize the University of Illinois Urbana-Champaign's (UIUC) growing commitment to urban public service. Through the efforts of an inspired and highly diverse group of faculty who believed that higher education, at its best, needed to go beyond the training of technically-skilled and commercially-successful students in order to cultivate individuals committed to using their education to insure that all Americans, but especially those living in grinding poverty in communities such as East St. Louis, have the opportunity to achieve our founding fathers' promise of "life, liberty, and the pursuit of happiness" and to work with others to realize Dr. King's ideal of "The Beloved Community".

This is the story of all of these people, leaders and participants from these communities, these students and others, and this is my story as well.

1. THE DECLINE OF EAST ST. LOUIS

WHEN I JOINED THE UNIVERSITY FACULTY in 1990, I never imagined that my entire UIUC career would focus on the struggles of a single distressed community, located nearly two hundred miles from our campus.

Sometime before I was hired, the university had launched a community-based research project in East St. Louis that UIUC's President Stanley O. Ikenberry had asked the planning department to initiate in collaboration with the College of Fine and Applied Arts' architecture and landscape architecture programs. The Urban Extension and Minority Access Program (UEMAP) was co-designed by Lew Hopkins, Head of the UIUC Department of Urban and Regional Planning, and Kieran Donaghy from the same department, in response to a stinging critique of the University offered by State Representative Wyvetter H. Younge (D-East St. Louis). She believed the campus was doing little, as Illinois' land grant university, to address the critical environmental, economic, and social problems confronting the state's rapidly declining African-American communities.

While Rep. Younge and other Illinois Legislative Black Caucus members had long complained about the university's somewhat anemic and highly selective extension efforts, her comments had taken on new importance given her recent appointment as chairperson of the legislature's powerful Higher Education Finance Committee.

During my first meeting with Lew Hopkins and Kieran Donaghy, they briefed me on the decline of East St Louis. This once-bustling port, railroad, manufacturing, retailing, and banking center had been devastated by the combined effects of suburbanization, disinvestment, and deindustrialization. Many long-time residents, business owners, and investors had abandoned the city. The city's business, employment, population, and revenue losses were exacerbated by the it's active participation in the federal government's public housing, urban renewal, and interstate highway programs that had resulted in additional displacement, demolition, out-migration and abandonment.

These and other forces, including the Reagan and Bush administration's supply-side economic and structural adjustment policies, had led to the loss of nearly three-quarters of the city's businesses and more than 12,000 well-paying jobs in its manufacturing, transportation, hospitality, and municipal services sectors between 1970 and 1990. These business and employment losses, along with growing racial tensions and residents' concerns regarding erosion in the quality of municipal services, especially schools, had caused the city's population to decline from 88,000 to 38,000 during this period. The majority of those leaving the city were working-class and middle-income whites who feared a collapse in the value of their homes, their family's most significant financial asset, and were anxious about living in a majority African-American community, having absorbed a lifetime of exposure to negative racial stereotypes featured in the news and popular culture.

The city's property tax base had shrunk from $600 million to $160 million during the 1970s and 1980s forcing local officials to repeatedly raise property taxes while drastically cutting basic services. Three out of every four tax dollars collected by East St. Louis in the late 1980s were being used to cover the costs of court-mandated judgment bonds for old debts when the city had defaulted. The city was too poor to pay its electric bills, leaving residents without street lights and traffic signals and forcing municipal officials to suspend trash collection prompting citizens to burn their garbage in violation of local and state laws or send their household rubbish to school with their children.

East St. Louis' mounting fiscal crisis had resulted in the termination of routine street and infrastructure maintenance; elimination of most afterschool, summer enrichment and employment training programs; closure of many neighborhood libraries, schools, playgrounds, and community/cultural centers; and frequently delayed and missed paychecks for municipal workers.

By the late 1980s, these and other examples of municipal failure prompted a senior HUD official to describe East St. Louis as the "most distressed small city in America" and a *St. Louis Post-Dispatch* editorial writer to label the city "America's Soweto." The city's school district, community college, housing authority, and Community Development Block Grant program had been put under various forms of state and federal receivership prompting the state legislature to draft the Financially Distressed Cities Law of 1990 that paved the way for a state takeover of the city's finances.

At the same time, there was a growing number of grassroots activists, institutional leaders (especially local pastors), neighborhood women and Rep. Younge committed to seizing control of their city's future through the launch of a citywide community development and municipal government reform movement. This emerging network of civic reformers had requested, through Rep. Younge's office, UIUC's assistance in designing a citywide community development strategy aimed at restoring the economic health and social vitality of this historic African-American city. The university's response was the Urban Extension and Minority Access Project (UEMAP).

When I joined the UIUC faculty, I had a strong belief in the potential of an interdisciplinary action research project to significantly strengthen the effectiveness of East St. Louis' resident-led organizing efforts. I understood participation in a well-structured field-based research program in a distressed community, such as East St. Louis, could have a powerful effect on the civic consciousness, critical-thinking, applied research skills, and professional values of students and faculty as well as the institution's understanding of its own role, as a land grant university, in a rapidly urbanizing state and nation.

Both my wife, Kathy, and I had grown up in working-class neighborhoods of New York City that had experienced devastating economic losses and physical decline in the 1960s and 1970s. The opportunity to play a role in the UEMAP partnership in East St. Louis was the most compelling aspect of the Assistant Professorship that UIUC had offered me. As Kathy said, "the job will give you the opportunity to use your community organizing experience and urban planning knowledge and skills to assist those who are in the greatest need. After all, isn't that why you became a planner?"

I had no idea of the life-transforming impact working for change in East St. Louis would have upon my future Illinois students, colleagues, and myself. Nor could I imagine the influence the project would have on UIUC's understanding of its land grant mission as well as other college and university administrators' expectations regarding the liberal education, institutional renewal, community development, and civic transformation potential of such projects!

2. THE LEGACY OF PAST COMMUNITY/ UNIVERSITY PARTNERSHIPS

WHEN I ARRIVED at the University of Illinois Urbana-Champaign in the summer of 1990, the UEMAP had been in place for two years, and was facing challenges. Its coordinator was the highly capable Carolyn Dry, Associate Professor in Architecture. Although her expertise in the field of material science had little connection to the issues confronting East St. Louis, she had volunteered to lead this effort when other UIUC faculty appeared unwilling to do so.

Professor Dry was motivated by Rep. Younge's compelling description of the daunting problems confronting East St. Louis residents. She subsequently persuaded Ernie Clay to join her. He was an experienced and highly regarded studio instructor and the school's only tenured African-American faculty member.

Between 1987 and 1990, Professors Dry and Clay recruited a small cadre of architecture, landscape architecture, and urban planning faculty to undertake research projects and design studios focused on many of East St. Louis' most serious urban problems. But convincing UIUC faculty to work in East St. Louis was a formidable challenge, notwithstanding the availability of $100,000 in annual support from the Provost's Office.

Faculty being considered for promotion and tenure were unsure how their involvement in the project would be evaluated within the university's increasingly competitive tenure and promotion process in which the number of peer-reviewed journal articles was viewed as the primary, and for some, the only relevant criterion for promotion. Others resisted participating in a community-based research project located 188 miles from campus.

For other faculty, the media's negative portrayal of East St. Louis as an environmentally hazardous, physically threatening, and politically corrupt community hostile to outsiders was sufficient to keep them away. Many white faculty with limited experience working in low-income minority communities, were reluctant to undertake projects requiring them to prepare students to navigate the many racial, class, gender, religious, and cultural differences between East St. Louis and the UIUC campus. Others, aware of the failure of many past UIUC extension efforts in low-income communities of color, including those in East St. Louis, did not want to become lightning rods for further resident criticism of the academy. Finally, sensitivity to issues of white privilege and institutional racism had been heightened by the university's recent refusal to abandon Chief Illiniwek (a fictive Native American leader) as its long-time athletic mascot, causing many faculty to avoid involvement in any project in which their attitudes and treatment of racial minorities could be challenged.

In spite of these obstacles, Professors Dry and Clay had encouraged a half dozen architecture, landscape architecture, and urban planning faculty to offer classes examining important East St. Louis issues of interest to Rep. Younge.

Beginning in the fall of 1987, Rep. Younge traveled to campus at the end of each semester to engage UEMAP students and faculty in spirited discussions regarding their latest East St. Louis research findings and policy recommendations. The best of these class-generated reports was published in the project's annual reports in 1988, 1989, and 1990. Among the topics examined in this series were: changing property ownership patterns along the East St. Louis waterfront; non-traditional approaches (above ground) to storm water management; municipal income, expenditures, and tax generation projections; municipal government re-organization options; economic and social benefits and costs of East St. Louis gaming; and the employment generation potential of manufactured housing for the Metro East Region.

Unfortunately, these reports generated little interest among local or state policy-makers. Only the casino gaming and manufactured housing studies gained traction. Those advocating state-sanctioned riverboat gambling in East St. Louis used Professor Clay's casino report. Professor Dry's manufactured housing study helped Rep. Younge secure a $900,000 Build Illinois Grant to establish a modular housing factory in the city that, unfortunately, failed.

When I arrived at UIUC, the lack of public and private sector interest in UEMAP's research projects, the logistical challenges of managing a long-distance extension effort, and the central

Historic entranceway sign to the City of East St. Louis (Photo by K. Reardon)

administration's failure to recognize their work had taken their toll on Professors Dry and Clay who were eager to transfer responsibility for managing the project to someone else. Me!

Professor Dry gave me two large boxes containing UEMAP project files, reference materials, annual reports, and an assortment of East St. Louis and Metro East maps and more. I began the work of carefully reviewing the mountain of East St. Louis historical documents, census data, news clippings, research reports, city plans and regional maps I had been given by both Professors Day and Clay. I also started to sift through the East St. Louis and St. Clair County documents contained in UIUC's impressive City Planning and Landscape Architecture Library.

It was here that I first discovered a battered copy of *The Plan for East St. Louis, Illinois* prepared in 1926 by legendary planner, Harland Bartholomew, who had also served as a longtime Adjunct Professor in UIUC's Department of Urban and Regional Planning. This remarkable document, prepared during a period of rapid growth within the St. Louis Region predicted, with great precision, the devastating impact unchecked suburbanization would have upon communities such as East St. Louis, located closest to the region's core.

I developed a database of local activists, business owners, institutional leaders, and elected officials who were involved in shaping the city's current economic and community development policies and plans. I hoped to interview these individuals regarding their perceptions of existing community conditions and future development opportunities prior to the start of the 1990-1991 academic year. During these interviews, I also planned to elicit their candid assessment of the past effectiveness and future potential of UIUC's East St. Louis project.

In the midst of this work Ishaq Shafiq, a second-year graduate planning student visited my office. Ishaq was born and raised in Chicago and had completed his BA in Political Science at UIUC several years prior. He had managed a variety of local economic development projects in Chicago while working for the Nation of Islam, and had directed a small home mortgage company in a rapidly expanding Atlanta suburb. For the past two years he had served as the department's UEMAP graduate research assistant.

Eager to benefit from the efforts of a graduate research assistant with community development experience in East St. Louis, I was thrilled to have Ishaq's help in preparing my upcoming Neighborhood Planning Workshop – a new course designed to support resident-led revitalization in East St. Louis.

We began our work together by combining the East St. Louis research materials generated by past UIUC students and faculty into an annotated bibliography that students enrolled in our fall class might find useful.

I subsequently started calling local leaders mentioned in past UEMAP reports and archival materials to request meetings to discuss their perceptions of current community conditions, ongoing development trends, alternative revitalization strategies, and the university's past, current, and possible future role supporting local economic development.

Between July and September of 1990, Ishaq and I logged more than 5,000 miles travelling between Champaign-Urbana and East St. Louis where we conducted more than forty interviews with a cross section of civic leaders, including officials, teachers, social service agency directors, church pastors, law enforcement officials, minority business owners, and journalists. We also interviewed more than a dozen faculty and staff from UIUC and nearby colleges and universities—people who had conducted community-based research, offered service-learning courses, or provided technical assistance to non-profit and government organizations serving East St. Louis.

A number of powerful themes emerged from this initial round of "movers and shakers" interviews. The severity of East St. Louis' economic and financial problems was repeatedly highlighted, along with the dramatic increase in the number of families requiring emergency food, shelter and other services. Many people described with considerable alarm, the spike in violent crime and drug-related deaths. Those we spoke to highlighted the city's growing inability to deliver police, fire, and sanitation services citing examples of police cars without radios, fire hydrants without water pressure and public works trucks without gasoline. Many of those we interviewed were especially concerned about the public safety and health threats posed by the city's loss of streetlights, traffic signals, and trash collection services. Many local leaders also discussed the stranglehold the East St. Louis and St. Clair County Democratic Organizations exerted over local government policy-making preventing the implementation of needed reforms and discouraging civic-minded residents from participating in the political process.

When asked their opinion of UIUC's UEMAP Project, those we interviewed were unaware of its existence! Asked to consider the potential contribution that a community-university development assistance project might make towards advancing resident-led planning and development in East St. Louis, interviewees appeared to be of one mind. The overwhelming majority believed that while colleges and universities did a good job providing undergraduates with a solid liberal arts education and graduate students with sound professional training, their repeated failure to provide effective support for the neighborhood revitalization efforts of poor and working-class families raised serious questions regarding the value of community-university development partnerships in cities such as East St. Louis. According to one interview, "We've been studied to death and what do we have to show for it?" Another interviewee stated, "The last thing East St. Louis needs is another university researcher who looks just like you, telling us what any sixth grader in town already knows and having the gall to charge us $100,000 in state funds for the privilege."

Only Bill Kreeb, executive director of the Lessie Bates Davis Neighborhood House, a one-hundred-year-old settlement house, located in the city's Emerson Park neighborhood showed any interest in working with UIUC. The Neighborhood House itself was providing support to a newly formed grassroots-organizing project—the Emerson Park Development Corporation (EPDC) whose members were committed to restoring their community one project at a time. I was delighted when Bill invited me to meet with staff—Ralph Mohammed, Director of Community Outreach, Louis Sweatt, Director of Social Work Services, and Ceola Davis, a long-time community outreach worker at the Neighborhood House—who were spearheading his agency's Emerson Park outreach efforts.

During our meeting, Ishaq and I learned a great deal about the neighborhood's rich history that began centuries before as a seasonal settlement for Mississippian Indians whose presence was still visible in the ceremonial mounds found throughout the neighborhood. The area had been transformed into a densely populated, working-class community in the early 20th century housing a diverse group of Eastern European workers attracted by the relatively well-paying jobs in the packinghouses, railyards, and chemical plants nearby.

Bill and his colleagues explained how East St. Louis experienced recurring economic and fiscal problems throughout its history due to Illinois' decision to allow local industries to create company towns beyond the city's municipal boundaries where they could limit their tax liabilities (and exercise greater control over labor). His staff also described the vibrant ethnic, religious, cultural and civic life that emerged in Emerson Park during the 1920s, 1930s, and 1940's around the neighborhood's many ethnically-based social clubs, fraternal organizations, labor unions, and Catholic Churches—the physical remnants of which were still visible in the decaying Packinghouse Workers of America Union Hall and the Slavic Society's buildings.

We were told that Post-World War II technological changes in the nation's meatpacking, chemical, pharmaceutical, and steel-making industries, in combination with the growing popularity of truck-based shipping, had destroyed the vast majority of jobs Emerson Park residents had historically depended upon. Bill's staff described how the closing of the Swift, Armour, and Morris meatpacking plants; the downsizing of the stockyards and its "spot market" auction and consolidation and downsizing of the city's rail yards in the 1950s and 1960s, had prompted most of the neighborhood's white ethnic population to leave the city in search of improved employment and entrepreneurial opportunities elsewhere.

Bill's staff explained that over time, the homes occupied by these families were either purchased or rented by African-American families attracted by the neighborhood's supply of handsome bungalows, tree-lined streets, low-crime rate, and strong sense of community. Sadly, the ongoing hemorrhaging of living wage jobs, the growing presence of African-American families, the block-busting activities of unscrupulous realtors who preyed upon white homeowners' racial fears, as well as the heightened fears of violence following the assassination of Dr. King in 1968 resulted in massive "white flight" from Emerson Park during the late 1960s through the mid-1970s.

The dramatic business, employment, and population losses described by the Neighborhood House staff had a crippling effect on the Emerson Park community between 1970 and 1990. During this period, total population within the neighborhood fell from 3,739 to 2,040, the African-American portion of the population rose from 65% to 98%, and the percentage of local families living in poverty skyrocketed from 19% to 78%. Visiting Emerson Park in the summer of 1990, Ishaq and I discovered that 40% of its building lots were vacant while 30% of its residential, commercial, civic, and industrial structures were abandoned—the vast majority of which were unsealed and deteriorating.

After chronicling the neighborhood's origins, growth, and decline, staff explained that the Neighborhood House Board had decided to support residents' efforts to establish a grassroots organizing, planning and development organization called the Emerson Park Development Corporation (EPDC). Davis, appeared to be the Neighborhood House's point person with EPDC, and she told us about a recent example of residents' organizing capacity.

A small group of neighborhood women, whose children attended the Neighborhood House's day care center, had become increasingly concerned about the impact the area's vacant, unattended lots and buildings were having on their children. They were particularly disturbed by the public safety threat posed by three abandoned, brick buildings that children attending the day care center had to pass by each day. These women, with Davis' help, used St. Clair County Tax Assessor's records to identify the owners of these properties. They were outraged when they discovered that the County, itself, held title to these properties following their owners' failure to pay their local property taxes. This discovery prompted the women to petition the County's Property Tax and Land Disposition Committee to transfer site control of these properties to EPDC so it could mobilize local volunteers and contractors to transform the offending properties into a "vest-pocket park" offering mothers, grandmothers, and other caregivers a safe, attractive, and comfortable place to interact with their children.

Davis and several neighborhood women had taken three buses from Emerson Park to the County Administration Building in suburban Belleville, Illinois to request site control of these properties in order to create a neighborhood playground. Armed with pictures of the properties and a map showing their proximity to the Neighborhood House's day care center, the women asked members of this powerful committee to give them title to these properties to enable them to create a safe space for children and mothers. Moved by the obvious commitment and sound arguments of these women, but concerned about the capacity of a newly formed organization, to redevelop and maintain these properties, the committee agreed to give temporary site control of these parcels to EPDC. However, they conditioned their approval on EPDC's ability to demolish the buildings clearing the site of all debris; prepare an acceptable site plan; and construct a playground consistent with city and county zoning, building, and property maintenance codes. They also required EPDC to secure liability coverage for those building and using the proposed facility and to submit a detailed management plan for the playground's future upkeep.

Encouraged by the County's willingness to support their playground proposal, EPDC mobilized dozens of residents to dismantle the existing three-story buildings on the site. They did this by hand, carefully saving recyclable materials including tin ceilings, lighting fixtures, bathroom and kitchen equipment, hardwood flooring, window and door units, copper wiring, and exterior bricks for resale. Over the course of several weeks, using little more than crowbars and elbow grease, EPDC "deconstructed" these structures creating a massive inventory of re-usable materials, which sold to antique dealers in St. Louis raising several thousand dollars.

Several residents launched a second fundraising initiative to support the playground's creation. Under the slogan, "Don't Cook Tonight—Call Ceola," they enlarged their construction "nest egg" by cooking $5 fried chicken and catfish dinners at the Neighborhood House on Friday evenings. One of the neighborhood women then suggested asking Ralston-Purina, whose world headquarters was visible from the neighborhood, to match the amount they had raised through their recycling and cooking campaigns.

The overwhelming majority of the neighborhood's households, businesses, churches, schools, and social service organizations worked together to level the playground site, install a perimeter sidewalk, construct park benches, plant a mix of annual and perennial flowers, erect a small water fountain, and install an entrance sign. Davis advised us that local residents had worked together during the past five years to maintain Shugue Park as a safe space for children and their caregivers, and the site had come to symbolize their shared commitment to reclaiming their community.

The community's success in creating Shugue Park had prompted EPDC's leaders to commit themselves to rebuilding Emerson Park lot-by-lot and block-by block. By doing so, they hoped to inspire the residents of other neighborhoods to undertake similar activities creating, over time, a citywide community renewal and civic reform movement. Realizing the complexity and scale of the projects they would have to undertake to "turn their neighborhood and city around"—EPDC's leaders were eager to establish a mutually beneficial partnership with students and faculty from nearby colleges and universities, including the University of Illinois at Urbana-Champaign. Deeply impressed by the extraordinary "bottom-up" planning and development campaign Emerson Park residents had undertaken to create a high-quality open space in their neighborhood, I was very eager to meet with leaders of this remarkable community-based development organization.

When Davis offered to arrange a meeting with EPDC and local faith-based leaders I quickly accepted, saying, "You tell me when and where to come, and Ishaq and I will be there." Ishaq and I returned to UIUC's Main Campus confident that we had identified the ideal East St. Louis organization as our partner.

3. OVERCOMING COMMUNITY SUSPICIONS

EAGER TO ESTABLISH A POSITIVE working relationship with a respected local organization before the fall semester started, I was extremely nervous about our upcoming meeting with EPDC. When Ishaq and I arrived at the Neighborhood House the following week, Ceola Davis escorted us to a lower-level conference room where she introduced us to five of EPDC's most active members—Anna Stevens, Kathy Tucker, Peggy Haney, James Peete, and Richard Suttle.

We were also introduced to Rev. Robert Jones, a local pastor who served as the Executive Director of the Metro East Area Project Board. Residents had invited him to the meeting to help them determine whether or not we were appropriate partners. We were interviewed, measured, and assessed.

Rev. Jones asked me to summarize my credentials, especially my experience, if any, working in low-income African-American communities. I was also asked to provide copies of recent reports or plans I had completed for any African-American communities where I had worked. In addition, he asked me for a list of African-American leaders from New York and New Jersey who could be contacted as references.

Rev. Jones also asked me to outline the rationale for the UEMAP and to describe the nature of UIUC's East St. Louis commitment. I told Rev. Jones and his neighbors that Rep. Younge's influence, as the newly appointed Chair of the state legislature's Higher Education Finance Committee was responsible for UIUC's interest in their community. I told them that I believed the project would last as long as Rep. Younge wielded substantial power within the state legislature and local residents supported the work being done by students and faculty. Rev. Jones asked me, "In the event, we move forward to establish a partnership with EPDC, other neighborhood institutions, and the university how would you envision getting started." I suggested we follow the advice of one of our profession's founders, the

Scottish botanist turned planner, Patrick J. Geddes, who consistently advised both lay and professional planners, "to survey before plan." Local residents and university planning students could work together to prepare a five-year stabilization plan to address the major factors causing ongoing outmigration of businesses, jobs, residents, and services from the neighborhood.

At this point one resident, rolling her eyes, responded by saying, "Honey, we've been studied to death!" While empathizing with this woman, I offered a number of reasons why I thought it made sense to begin our partnership by working together to co-produce a comprehensive plan. I pointed out that East St. Louis' existing master plan was more than twenty years old and focused little attention on the revitalization needs of its older residential neighborhoods such as Emerson Park. I also explained how public agencies responsible for local economic and community development funding were becoming increasingly interested in projects formulated as part of overall plans or strategies, rather than as single stand-alone initiatives. In addition, many local residents, business owners, and institutional leaders, weary of the city's long history of corruption and backroom deal-making, would be more likely to view projects identified through an empirically grounded and highly democratic planning process as legitimate and worthy of support. Finally, I stressed that private funders, including area foundations and corporations, aware of the city's history of mismanagement would be unlikely to give serious consideration to any local redevelopment project, regardless of how worthy it might be, in the absence of a carefully prepared, empirically based, and resident supported plan.

While still eager to focus on the EPDC list of immediate revitalization projects, the group accepted my arguments for producing an asset-based stabilization plan focused on the most serious causes of neighborhood disinvestment, out-migration, and abandonment. But it still wasn't clear if UIUC had been accepted as a partner. As we made our way toward the door, Rev. Jones invited those present to bow their heads in prayer. Feeling hands on my shoulders I was moved to hear him ask God to provide Ishaq and I with "travelling mercies" to keep us safe during our long drive home. During the next ten years, UIUC students and faculty working in East St.

Louis rarely left the city without receiving similar blessings. I was always deeply touched to receive such blessings from East St. Louis residents—marveling at their concern for us as we navigated our way home on well-engineered highways in late model university vans while they, on the other hand, often walked home, in small groups after EPDC/UEMAP events along streets that, in a heartbeat, could turn deadly.

Lew Hopkins, head of the UIUC Department of Urban and Regional Planning, strongly encouraged me to pursue a partnership with the EPDC. Davis soon confirmed EPDC's strong interest in working with us. But we still had to negotiate the details of the partnership.

The following week, Ishaq and I returned to the Neighborhood House where we met with Davis, Rev. Jones, and their EPDC colleagues. At this meeting, we were confronted with the legacy of many past failed partnerships.

As was so often the case, Davis began the meeting. She pointed to three stacks of reports lying in the middle of the conference table where we had gathered—all university-generated research studies describing economic conditions and future revitalization possibilities for East St. Louis completed in the 1960s, 1970s, and 1980s. The overwhelming majority of the findings contained in these reports highlighted the city's many deficits while giving little, if any, attention to East St. Louis' significant assets. According to those attending the meeting, these reports had contributed to a widely held perception of their city as a terminal case of urban decline—a view of East St. Louis held by many influential regional leaders that had made it extremely difficult for local organizations to secure external funding even for the most worthwhile revitalization projects!

According to Davis, very few of the economic and community development proposals featured in these reports had ever been implemented, but the UIUC faculty who had prepared these documents had been paid to do so using the considerable overhead these projects generated to cover the costs of summer salaries for faculty, graduate research assistantships, and campus equipment and facilities.

While emphasizing EPDC's strong desire to enter into a productive partnership with UIUC, Davis stated that she and her neighbors were not willing to do so on a "business as usual" basis in which the campus reaped the lion's share of the partnership benefits while the community realized few, if any, advantages while being saddled with considerable additional responsibilities and costs.

EPDC's leaders then presented us with a list of principles for the establishment of non-exploitative, mutually beneficial, community-university development partnerships in East St. Louis. Over the years, we came to refer to these values as the Ceola Accords.

1. Local residents and stakeholders rather than the university, their funders, or local officials will determine the issues the partnership works on.

2. Local residents and leaders will be fully engaged as equal partners, with university-trained professionals, at each step of the planning process from issue identification to program implementation and project evaluation.

3. University partners will make a minimum five-year commitment to the partnership beyond an initial probationary year to insure that improvement projects identified by the project can be advanced from conceptualization to implementation.

4. University partners will recognize the significant costs that community-based research and collaborative planning projects impose on local institutions by making a consistent effort to include resources for local capacity building in all of their external funding proposals.

5. University partners will work with neighborhood activists and citywide leaders to establish a community-based and resident-controlled development organization to be responsible for the successful implementation of long-term planning and development efforts in light of what appears to be a short-term commitment to the city by the university.

Rev. Jones emphasized that local leaders viewed many university faculty who worked in East St. Louis as little more than "carpetbaggers," who used the city's extreme poverty to secure grants providing benefits for themselves and their universities while offering little, if any, support to local residents and institutions. He stressed how strongly local leaders felt about the need to establish and maintain reciprocity and equity within any proposed partnership. He also described the political risks local residents and leaders were taking, in light of the long history of abuse that East St. Louis had suffered at the hands of self-serving "hit and run researchers" and "windshield sociologists." In the minds of many residents and leaders, Davis and her EPDC colleagues, would be viewed as "sell-outs" or "dupes" for entering into another partnership with a powerful, white-controlled institution, such as UIUC, given its checkered history within the community.

Since Davis and her neighbors were putting their considerable social capital on the line, the EPDC was demanding a radically different model of community-university collaboration—one based upon mutual respect, shared commitment and risk, and joint payoff.

Returning to campus, Ishaq and I discussed the principles for non-exploitative partnerships with Lew Hopkins, Professors Dry and Clay, as well as several other faculty members who had participated in UEMAP's past initiatives. With few exceptions, these individuals understood the residents' concerns regarding the lack of transparency and reciprocity within past UIUC-sponsored outreach and research efforts. These individuals supported the residents' call for a more democratic and equitable approach to community planning and development within the city. Following these discussions, we subsequently wrote a letter to EPDC committing ourselves to adhering to the spirit and letter of their proposed accords.

The tentative plan was to begin working with EPDC's leaders to formulate a comprehensive neighborhood stabilization plan that addressed the most important issues confronting this historic community. We planned to use participatory action research methods to produce this plan which would actively involve local residents and stakeholders, on an equal basis with university-trained professionals, at each step in the planning process from problem identification to project implementation to program evaluation.

A small group of planning students had enrolled in my neighborhood planning workshop and would be available to work with EPDC's leaders in preparing an asset-based stabilization plan for Emerson Park between August and December of 1990. Hoping to earn Emerson Park residents' and leaders' respect as committed and skilled advocacy planners, capable of supporting their stabilization and revitalization efforts, we intended to build upon our initial "bottom-up" planning initiative to support residents in their subsequent efforts to implement a series of increasingly challenging neighborhood improvement projects.

I subsequently prepared a preliminary Memorandum of Understanding for EPDC's leaders and Davis to review, that presented the goals and objectives of our community planning/ development partnership, activities to be carried out as part of the neighborhood planning process, and description of the partnership's primary short-term deliverable (i.e. five-year stabilization plan). The next step was to identify key participants and their roles, and a tentative timetable.

Following the successful negotiation of an MOU between EPDC and the University, we would need a steering committee comprised of EPDC and other community-based organizations serving the Emerson Park neighborhood. The Steering Committee's role would be to oversee the development and implementation of the plan; encourage skeptical local stakeholders to participate in the process; serve as spokespersons for the effort; and defend the partnership against the attacks of local elites likely to be threatened by a highly democratic planning process. We would work with the soon-to-be-appointed steering committee to design and execute an aggressive community-based media campaign to inform Emerson Park stakeholders about the process and to invite those most inter- ested in insuring its success to assume leadership roles within our fledgling effort.

Ceola Davis soon confirmed EPDC's endorsement of our pre- liminary proposal. Ishaq and I then returned to the Neighborhood House and in a meeting with the leaders, we signed a two-page MOU outlining the goals, objectives, activities, timetable, and deliverables related to the production of our proposed stabilization plan. We also took time to examine a large East St. Louis base map to establish the boundaries for our proposed Emerson Park planning and development activities. Together we identified local residents, business owners, and institutional leaders, including area school teachers, principals, pastors, and non-profit executives, representative of the neighborhood's diversity to serve on the soon-to-be-established steering committee.

EPDC's executive committee volunteered to recruit these individuals and we agreed to convene the first meeting of the steering committee in two weeks to revisit the MOU, review the steps and schedule for the proposed neighborhood planning process, agree upon a community-based media campaign, organize a neighborhood orientation for participating UIUC students and faculty, and decide upon a date for a "kick-off event" for the planning process. Everyone agreed that the event should take place shortly after the start of the school year so notices could be sent to parents via their children.

Two weeks later, Ishaq and I returned to the Neighborhood House to meet with a group of twelve neighborhood leaders recruited for the steering committee. The group included several EPDC Executive Committee representatives, Lessie Bates Davis Neighborhood House staff, Ninth Street Public Housing Resident Association members, East St. Louis Senior Citizen Council representatives, three local business owners, a Catholic Charities official, and a long-time homeless man with an encyclopedic knowledge of the area's history, buildings, organizations, and residents. With this group's help, we formulated a multi-pronged strategy for informing local stakeholders about the planning effort and established dates for both the student orientation and the official "kick-off" event for the process.

Buoyed by Davis' enthusiasm and her neighbors' obvious commitment to the effort, Ishaq and I returned to campus eager to use the remaining time before the fall term to maximize enrollment in our neighborhood planning workshop whose students, unbeknownst to them, would be working in East St. Louis' Emerson Park neighborhood.

4. THE EMERSON PARK NEIGHBORHOOD IMPROVEMENT PLAN

RETURNING FROM EAST ST. LOUIS, Ishaq and I worked hard to promote our newly developed class as an exciting experiential learning opportunity for those seeking to enhance their community development knowledge and skills. Thanks to an aggressive bulletin board campaign and colleagues who encouraged their students to "Check out UP 387" two undergraduates and nine graduate students attended our first neighborhood planning workshop class.

I began the class by retelling Ceola Davis' story about how a small group of Emerson Park women transformed three of East St. Louis' most environmentally-challenged properties into a beautifully designed mini-park, prompting their neighbors to commit themselves to reclaiming their neighborhood one parcel at a time. I concluded my remarks by explaining how EPDC, the organization established by these women, had requested the university's assistance and how, if they chose to remain in the class, they could be part of this exciting new community development assistance project! Hoping to encourage them to stick with the class, I stressed the transformative impact working with such committed community leaders could have on their careers and lives.

Not wanting to have students in the class who were unwilling to roll their sleeves up, I also highlighted some of the obstacles we would likely face working in a city where political deals routinely trumped professional plan making. Among the challenges I cited was the distance separating our campus and Emerson Park; the lack of current conditions data; the deteriorated infrastructure that could make fieldwork hazardous; escalating violence among local drug dealers struggling to expand their turf; and domination of local government by an eighty-year-old political machine. Following these remarks, I invited the students to take a short break to reconsider their participation in the class which I told them would require significantly more work than their other courses. Ishaq and I were delighted when all eleven students returned to class following the break.

The following week, I made the first of many visits to UIUC's fleet garage to sign-out a fifteen-passenger van to take the students on the three-and-a-half-hour trip to East St. Louis. Shortly after turning on to I-55/70 South, Ishaq distributed copies of the MOU that we had co-developed with the newly formed steering committee for an Emerson Park Neighborhood Improvement Plan. It outlined our project's goals and objectives, major activities, community and university roles, proposed timetable, and deliverable (i.e. the production of a professional-quality neighborhood stabilization plan). The students read the document with great interest, especially its scope of services section that specified the activities they would be responsible for completing during the next sixteen weeks.

This scope of services included the following activities:

1. Collection and analysis of past studies, reports, and plans focused on improving the quality of life within the Emerson Park neighborhood.

2. Collection and analysis of recent population, employment/income, and housing data for the Emerson Park neighborhood from the U.S. Census.

3. Completion of a preliminary "windshield survey" of community assets, including: important natural features, historic sites, public facilities, non-profit service organizations, and private businesses serving the community.

4. Engagement of local stakeholders in a community mapping exercise to verify the neighborhood's boundaries and identify what residents perceived to be the area's most important assets, challenges, and untapped resources.

5. Implementation of a field survey of current land uses, building conditions, parcel maintenance levels, and infrastructure conditions within the neighborhood.

6. Execution of a series of "movers and shakers" interviews with local leaders to elicit their views regarding current conditions, future development options, and needed planning interventions.

7. Completion of a similar set of interviews regarding current conditions, future development options, and desired planning interventions with local residents.

8. Summary of major research findings using Stanford Research International's Strengths, Weaknesses, Opportunities, and Threats (SWOT) Analysis Framework.

9. Formal presentation of a preliminary draft of a five-year stabilization plan for community review, revision, and approval.

10. Finalization of the stabilization plan based upon community feedback to be presented and adopted by the East St. Louis City Council as an amendment to the city's existing comprehensive plan.

One of the students asked, "How can we possibly accomplish all of this during one semester?" I suggested we make bi-weekly trips to East St. Louis following our Thursday classes, returning to Champaign late Friday evenings. In this way, we could devote a full eight plus hour day, every other week to East St. Louis fieldwork. Ishaq and I would be travelling to Emerson Park in between these field trips to collect additional materials, hold meetings with local residents, and canvass the neighborhood prior to community meetings. For the next two hours conversation filled the van as students and faculty got to know one another while discussing various aspects of our project.

Upon entering the city, the van became extremely quiet as students noted a poorly maintained municipal park and sports facility, numerous abandoned industrial complexes, and a vast underutilized rail yard surrounded by the skeletal structures of former warehouses. Exiting the interstate in downtown East St. Louis, the students immediately observed the lack of functioning traffic lights, missing street signs, overflowing trash receptacles, and a large number of vacant retail spaces and commercial offices. Turning onto Collinsville Avenue, one of the downtown's major east-west commercial corridors, they were shocked to see pigeon's flying out of the city's tallest structure—the historic Spivey Gas and Electric Building.

As we crossed I-64, Ishaq informed the class that we had just entered Emerson Park. By this time, you could hear a pin drop! The students were, as Ishaq and I had previously been, overwhelmed by the ravaged state of this once-vibrant city, formerly known as "The Pittsburgh of the West". As we approached the Neighborhood House, Rich Koenig, one of the graduate students who had previously lobbied me to come to UIUC, asked, "How can we possibly help these folks?" I responded by saying, "I am not quite sure, but, from the looks of things the only direction to go is up!" At this point Davis emerged from Neighborhood House. Opening the van's side door, she greeted our group with a warm smile stating, "Good afternoon and welcome to Emerson Park!"

Davis explained to the EPDC's executive committee how our class would be working with them, the steering committee and the settlement house staff to prepare a comprehensive stabilization plan. I then distributed the preliminary EPDC/UIUC MOU for all to review. Acknowledging the ambitious nature of the work plan, I told the students that I was confident in their ability to complete a high-quality neighborhood stabilization plan by the end of the semester. At that point, Suttle, who possessed an uncanny ability to offer humorous comments designed to set people at ease, said, "Professor Reardon, that is easy for you to say, but they are going to be doing all of the work".

Davis invited us to join her for a walking tour of the neighborhood. Leaving the Neighborhood House, we encountered a group of young children who were heading home from the day care program. As we left the group, Davis said, "In the end, helping these babies become caring adults is what this work is all about." Turning to the students she said, "We are counting on you to produce a plan that will help our community which faces so many challenges support these children—each of whom deserve better!"

We then headed down an alley across from the neighborhood's largest housing complex where a group of men were gathered around an open fire. As we approached, Davis introduced us to the group as her new friends from the U of I who would be working in the neighborhood. At this point, a young man named Ed, stepped forward offering to help us in any way he could. As we headed towards the public housing project, Davis reminded the men that she would be serving dinner at the Neighborhood House at 3 PM on Sunday. She later explained how she and several other EPDC women prepared home cooked meals every Sunday for those who were homeless or without families. We subsequently learned that Davis had been preparing and funding these weekly dinners out of her modest Neighborhood House salary for many years.

During the ride home, the students raised dozens of questions regarding Emerson Park, the city, and its future. A good deal of this discussion focused on what we could reasonably accomplish during a single semester to advance EPDC's redevelopment efforts. After considerable discussion, the students concluded that they could, with a great deal of effort and a bit of luck, document Emerson Park's long history of resident-led revitalization. They also believed they could help EPDC expand its membership base and leadership group thereby enhancing its organizational capacity. Finally, they felt they could produce an evidence-based stabilization plan that could begin to address the major factors contributing to the neighborhood's continued disinvestment, out-migration, and abandonment. If EPDC were successful in stabilizing the neighborhood using such a plan, they believed subsequent five-year plans co-produced by local residents and other university planners could advance more ambitious citywide revitalization strategies.

After reviewing our preliminary scope of services, the students organized themselves into four teams focused on archival research, demographic analysis, community mapping, and project communications. In the days following our trip, they scoured UIUC's City Planning and Landscape Architecture Library for East St. Louis materials. They also began extracting recent population, employment, income, poverty, and housing data for the city, St. Clair County, and Illinois from the census. In addition, they reached out to East St. Louis officials and regional librarians to secure an accurate base map for the neighborhood. They also worked with EPDC's leaders to prepare a press release describing the Emerson Park planning process for distribution to local news outlets. In addition, they developed a short letter introducing the project to local institutional leaders, including church pastors and school principals, encouraging them to join the effort. Finally, they devised a second introduction letter to be distributed door-to-door to local residents inviting them to the project's upcoming "kick-off" meeting.

The following week Ishaq and I returned to Emerson Park with six students to meet with EPDC's executive committee and the steering committee for an Emerson Park Improvement Plan to review the agenda for our first community planning forum. While Ishaq and I met with these groups, our students conducted a "windshield tour" of the community identifying and mapping local public facilities, historic landmarks, and various problem spots where illegal dumping, building abandonment, and illicit drug sales appeared to be taking place.

Following our meeting with local leaders and the students' neighborhood survey, we met six community volunteers who had agreed to assist us in canvassing the neighborhood in preparation for our upcoming meeting. While the students and their community partners door-knocked the neighborhood's 350 occupied housing units, Ishaq and I field-checked the accuracy of the Emerson Park base map we had been given by the city—a twenty-five-year-old document. While the map was, for the most part, accurate, it contained a number of discrepancies. For example, the map featured several streets located at the northwestern edge of the neighborhood that seemed to have disappeared. Local residents subsequently explained how individuals struggling to make ends meet would often "mine the urban environment". They would visit brick paved streets where homes were abandoned with crowbars to remove the beautifully aged paving stones reselling them to local antique dealers whose customers valued their durability, worn edges, and lovely patina. We also discovered two housing complexes, one occupied and one unoccupied, that did not appear on the city's base map.

On the return trip to campus the students reported, without exception, that the canvassing had gone exceptionally well. They were also eager to share what they had learned about the neighborhood from the residents. On the positive side, many residents described the neighborhood's rich immigrant, labor, and civil rights history; civic-minded residents, educators, pastors, and social service directors; quiet streets and attractive bungalow houses. On the negative side, residents discussed their disappointment with local schools, deteriorating infrastructure, declining public services, escalating street violence, ongoing out-migration, and illegal dumping. While the residents appeared to be deeply concerned about their neighborhood's future, they were unsure as to what, if anything, they could do to turn their community and city around.

The students spent the two weeks following this trip preparing for our first community planning forum that was scheduled to take place at the Neighborhood House. The class developed a "historical timeline" they hoped residents would help them fill in to better understand and communicate Emerson Park's evolution. They also created a community facilities and assets map showing the locations of various community resources and landmarks they hoped people attending the meeting would help them further develop. Finally, they prepared a set of large display boards comparing recent economic, demographic and housing trends in Emerson Park with those of East St. Louis, St. Clair County, and Illinois that they planned to present to the residents.

After discussing the kick-off meeting with the steering committee, the students decided to make the first community planning forum as interactive as possible by limiting local officials' comments and reports to a minimum, preserving as much time as possible for local stakeholders to share their concerns and improvement proposals with each other. As we approached the Neighborhood House on the night of the forum, we were thrilled to see a full parking lot and groups of people entering the building. Entering the gym, the class was delighted to see more than forty children and adults, many of whom they had met while door knocking, eagerly waiting the start of the meeting.

Following a short welcome from the Neighborhood House's Bill Kreeb, Anna Stevens, chair of the steering committee for an Emerson Park Neighborhood Improvement Plan, thanked everyone for coming and explained the importance of combining everyone's best ideas and efforts to get Emerson Park back on its feet. She described how EPDC and its supporters would be working with the university to identify and address the major challenges facing the neighborhood. Following these remarks, Davis explained how Rep. Younge had invited the university to assist community residents and elected officials working for change in East St. Louis. She concluded her remarks by thanking Bill Kreeb for encouraging UIUC to launch their East St. Louis efforts in Emerson Park.

I introduced our student team to the audience, which responded with enthusiastic applause. Thanking the residents for their warm welcome, I told them how honored we were to be working in a historic neighborhood such as theirs where residents had already done so much to improve their community. Highlighting their recent success in creating Shugue Park, I told them we were committed to doing all we could to support their ongoing revitalization efforts.

My students had laid out their sparsely populated historic timeline at the back of the gym, and the residents, including the children, added the events they believed had been most influential in shaping the neighborhood. Residents mentioned the opening of the stockyards, construction of the Gompers public housing project, launch of the Packinghouse Workers Organizing Committee, passage of Illinois' annexation legislation, construction of interstates 55/70 and 64, and many other events which our students were excited to add to the timeline.

In small groups residents were then invited to identify, locate, and describe Emerson Park's most important assets. Working in these groups, residents quickly rattled off lists of positive community assets, including Emerson Park's location, highway access, housing stock, religious institutions, street system, public schools, and landmarks. As residents mentioned and described these attributes, the student facilitators, with the assistance of student "recorders," located, labeled, and annotated each asset on large base maps at each table using thick green markers.

The student facilitators then asked residents to identify the major problems facing the neighborhood. In a relatively short period of time, dangerous intersections, missing manhole covers, broken traffic lights, abandoned buildings, unkempt lots, illegal dumping sites, and drug "hotspots" were identified and noted on the large base maps with red markers. Finally, residents were asked to locate on the large base maps with purple markers their neighborhoods' greatest untapped resources which prompted individuals at nearly every table to circle the recently closed Cannady School that many felt could be cost-effectively transformed into an adult education, job training, drug treatment, or senior housing complex. At the end of this activity, we invited the residents to stand for a quick stretch to note the hundreds of red, green, and purple entries they and their neighbors had generated. We explained how our class would be working during the coming weeks to transform their observations into a preliminary neighborhood conditions report that would, along with the historic timeline, serve as the introduction to the Emerson Park Neighborhood Improvement Plan.

Students then shared with forum participants the results of their initial analysis of neighborhood economic and demographic trends. While residents were familiar with the general population, education, employment/income, and housing trends the students described, they were shocked to see just how badly Emerson Park compared to the city and the county. As the students completed their presentation, Ed, the young man we had met during our walking tour, jumped to his feet. He began his remarks by complimenting the students on their hard work. He then asked why they had not included a comparison of Emerson Park's economic and demographic trends with those of the surrounding suburban communities that comprised the non-East St. Louis portion of the county. According to Ed, "By comparing Emerson Park with the city and the county you fail to capture the dramatic income and wealth disparities separating East St. Louis from its suburban neighbors. This happens because your current comparison communities contain so many poor people from East St. Louis." He encouraged them to add one more column to their charts containing data for suburban St. Clair. "If you don't do this, your data will never reveal the 'Tale of Two Cities' that you experience when travelling into the city from the adjacent suburbs."

Not sure how to respond to Ed's gently presented but damning critique of their preliminary report, the students turned to me in hopes of being rescued. I responded by saying, "Ed, you are absolutely right! Your suggestion would significantly improve our analysis. We will definitely add the suburban St. Clair comparison you've recommended." Following this brief exchange, we did a quick meeting evaluation during which people complimented the students on their meeting preparations, presentations, and facilitation. Before leaving, Davis encouraged those attending the meeting to assist the class in carrying out its upcoming land use/physical conditions survey and to help the steering committee in increasing attendance at the next meeting.

Heading back to Champaign, the students shared their excitement regarding the meeting. They were moved to see so many of the people they had spoken to while door knocking at the event. They were also delighted by the way in which the residents actively participated in the meeting enthusiastically contributing to the historic timeline and community mapping exercises. Their only negative comments focused on Ed's critique of their census work and my failure to better prepare and defend them from his "attack." Apologizing for not anticipating the value of including the suburban "collar towns" in our analysis, I told them they should be delighted that someone took their work seriously enough to offer a meaningful and thoughtful critique. "We do participatory planning because we don't know everything. History, culture, and context are all important in planning. Since we are usually functioning as 'outsiders' albeit well-intentioned ones in the communities where we work, we must depend upon local actors, such as Ed, to fill in what are often breathtaking gaps in our knowledge and understanding."

During the next week, the class revised their census analysis, completed the Emerson Park historical timeline, and prepared a community mapping report based upon the residents' input. Meanwhile, Ishaq and I worked on the development of a methodology for analyzing basic environmental, infrastructure, and housing conditions based upon survey instruments contained in F. Stuart Chapin's classic *Land Use Planning* text. Eager to collect data that would produce an accurate description of existing physical conditions, including, residents' ongoing efforts to improve their properties, we added a number of variables not typically contained in mainstream land use surveys to avoid being another group of researchers who highlighted obvious community deficiencies at the expense of important assets. As a result, we incorporated a landscape improvement variable to capture residents' ongoing beautification efforts as well as a recent housing investment variable to highlight residents' exterior building improvements.

Two weeks later, the class accompanied by several additional student volunteers returned to Emerson Park for our first multi-day fieldwork effort. During the next several hours, our students and eight community partners struggled with the Sidwell Map Company's challenging notation system for recording property information, less-than-clear local maps, and our "not quite ready for prime time" survey instrument, using all three tools in an effort to collect reliable data regarding the neighborhood's physical conditions. By the time they returned to the Neighborhood House at the end of their first full day of fieldwork, they were feeling pretty good about their newly acquired surveying skills.

Rising early the next day, we repeated our first day's routine stopping at the Neighborhood House to meet a second group of community volunteers ready to help us complete the survey. By the end of our second day, we had inspected all of the 1,407 building parcels comprising the Emerson Park study area—a feat we took great pride in having accomplished. I congratulated them on a job well done before reluctantly informing them that they would soon learn the real meaning of their MCP degrees. Many people referred to the Master of City and Regional Planning degree as the Master of Colored Pencils degree in light of the inordinate amount of time planning students and professionals spend hand-coloring maps in the days before smart phones, laptops, and GIS software packages.

By the end of the following week, the class had enlisted their "significant and insignificant others," including boy/girlfriends, fellow graduate planning students, as well as a several curious architecture and landscape architecture majors to render their physical conditions maps which they proudly displayed in the foyer of the Department of Urban and Regional Planning.

While the students were working hard to complete their land use, building conditions, and site maintenance maps, Ishaq and I were busy reviewing the planning and civil engineering literatures for an easy-to-use but reliable methodology for assessing neighborhood infrastructure conditions. While most American cities have well-staffed engineering departments, supported by a variety of consultants, to monitor important elements of their built environment, this was not the case in East St. Louis in 1990. When our literature search failed to surface a workable methodology for conducting a neighborhood infrastructure survey, we designed one.

The following week, our class travelled to East St. Louis to conduct a street-section-by-street-section survey of the neighborhood's aboveground infrastructure. During this effort, they mapped infrastructure elements that were missing (i.e. a sidewalk panel or street name sign), the location of all streetlights, as well as the materials used and condition of the streets, sidewalks, and curbing.

A week later, the class returned to Emerson Park for a second community planning forum that attracted approximately fifty residents. Following a welcome, a few introductions, and a quick review of the agenda by Davis, the students presented their revised census analysis that had been modified to include the additional comparison Ed had recommended. The students noted how dramatic the disparities in income, poverty, and housing conditions were when one compared Emerson Park's population and housing trends with those of the suburban "collar towns" as Ed had suggested. Looking at the back of the room, I saw Ed smiling as he whispered to those sitting near him that he had to "straighten the professor out on this one." Three members of the class then presented the results of our recently completed land use, building conditions, and lot maintenance survey.

Following their presentation of local building conditions, residents encouraged the students to examine the ownership of the so-called "problem properties" that had been identified. They believed that the vast majority of these parcels were owned by various municipal and county agencies and a small number of absentee slumlords. A subsequent review of Emerson Park's property ownership records supported the residents' claim that the vast majority of homeowner properties were in good to excellent repair while the overwhelming majority of governmentally and absentee-owned units were in poor to very poor condition.

During their presentation, the students pointed out the high percentage of local homeowners who had made significant improvements to their properties, including: the installation of new roofs, doors, and windows; construction of patios, decks, garages and decorative fences; and the planting of trees, shrubs, and flowers. Discussing these improvements, residents reminded the class that these improvements were, with few exceptions, self-financed because local banks, until very recently, had refused to make home improvement and/or mortgage loans, regardless of the credit worthiness of local families, in the city's poor and working-class neighborhoods.

The students also presented the highlights of their local infrastructure survey. It revealed a mixed picture. The majority of the streets, curbs, sidewalks, storm drains, and streetlights at the heart of the neighborhood were in very good shape; however, most of the street name and traffic signs as well as the manhole covers throughout the neighborhood were missing. The infrastructure at the neighborhood's periphery was much more distressed. In these areas, sections of streets and curbing had been removed making it impossible to safely drive through these areas. There were also a large number of illegal dumpsites where perpetrators didn't bother to leave their loads in alleys or on the side of the roads.

Residents explained how commercial garbage trucks eager to escape escalating "tipping fees" at nearby landfills routinely drove their vehicles into the neighborhood's most sparsely populated areas where they dropped their garbage. One local resident described how he solved this problem on his street, "When the driver stopped in front of my house to drop a load, I jumped up on his running board with my favorite hunting rifle suggesting he take his load somewhere else. We haven't seen this guy or any of his friends since." Seeking a less dangerous solution to the illegal dumping problem, a resident asked if our students could collect samples of mail with intact addresses from the larger illegal dumpsites. With addresses revealing the source of the garbage, he hoped the county prosecutor or U.S. Attorney for the Southern District of Illinois could pursue the unscrupulous haulers responsible for Emerson Park's illegal dumping crisis.

Near the end of the meeting, we informed the residents that we would be completing our local data collection efforts with a series of "movers and shakers" interviews with local officials and as many resident interviews as we could complete. We invited those present to comment on the preliminary list of local officials we planned to interview and the questions we intended to ask them.

The residents were pleased to see so many influential public and private funders on our list. They were very eager to hear what these individuals had to say about Emerson Park and its future. They were especially curious to learn what, if anything, these leaders were prepared to do to support stabilization efforts in neighborhoods such as Emerson Park. But they asked why we needed to ask residents what the neighborhood's biggest problems were given the significant amounts of data we had already collected regarding these issues. I explained that we needed to support our analysis of existing conditions and recommended policy proposals with as many different forms of data as possible. "People are not expecting a high-quality plan from East St. Louis. One of the legacies of the city's long history of corruption is that anything with an East St. Louis label on it is, quite frankly, viewed with great skepticism. We simply can't afford to give any potential public and private investor a reason to ignore your neighborhood and its needs."

Before adjourning the meeting, we again asked people to share their evaluation of the meeting with us. After complimenting us on the quality of our presentations and meeting facilitation, several residents encouraged us to send copies of the most important meeting handouts to residents prior to these events. "In this way, we can review these materials before the meetings and provide you with better input," remarked Kathy Tucker, one of EPDC's most active members.

During the next two weeks, Ishaq and I scheduled more than thirty "movers and shakers" interviews with local leaders. Before these interviews, we introduced the students to the fundamentals of face-to-face interviewing using William Foote Whyte's *Learning From The Field: A Guide From Experience* and organized simulated practice interviews reflecting potential friendly, indifferent and hostile interviewees. With the help of several neighborhood leaders, we managed to complete thirty-two interviews with local officials.

Among the most shocking observations from these interviews were the large number of officials who could not locate Emerson Park on a map. Local leaders' strongly held view was that there was little the city could do to halt the decline of its neighborhoods, and their widely held belief that the state and federal governments would ultimately rescue East St. Louis. When pressed to provide planning and policy recommendations to address the decline of Emerson Park and other residential neighborhoods in the city, the interviewees offered a number of proposals, beyond those already being pursued by local anti-poverty agencies. Among these were:

1. A campaign should be undertaken by the city to recover property and equipment that former and current municipal employees had looted.

2. An effort should be initiated by the city to more effectively collect the back taxes local property owners, especially absentee landlords, have failed to pay.

3. A "buy-local" program requiring city, school district, and city-funded non-profits to increase the percentage of goods and services they purchase from local businesses should be launched.

4. Future East St. Louis police officers, firemen, and schoolteachers should be required to live in the city.

5. State legislation to enable a "residency" tax requiring those working in East St. Louis while living elsewhere to pay a small per capita levy to support local services should be pursued.

6. A local ordinance requiring absentee property owners to provide the city with basic identification information to enable them to be held accountable for the maintenance of their local properties should be pursued.

7. State legislation forbidding bond-for-deed and/or land contracts for use outside of agricultural, commercial, and industrial properties, should be developed and passed.

8. The passage of state legislation allowing riverboat gambling in East St. Louis should be considered.

Following the completion of this work, the class accompanied by a half-a-dozen other student volunteers travelled to East St. Louis for three days to interview as many Emerson Park residents as possible. With the assistance of local leaders, we were able to interview more than 140 heads of households. With few exceptions, local residents invited our interviewers into their homes. For the vast majority of the residents, this was the first time their opinions on local affairs had ever been solicited, and they appeared eager to share their views on current conditions and future development possibilities.

The overwhelming majority had very positive feelings about Emerson Park. They described how quiet the neighborhood tended to be, the quality of the housing stock, its proximity to local schools, the range of services available at the Neighborhood House, and the strong sense of community that existed among residents. They also expressed their concerns regarding issues that could further destabilize the neighborhood. The residents were alarmed by recent increase in street violence attributed to competition among local drug dealers for control of the lucrative crack-cocaine trade. Residents were also concerned about the environmental hazards confronting local families, especially children—the missing manhole covers, vacant and open structures, and accumulations of illegally dumped trash. Interviewees also mentioned the shortage of living wage jobs for those without private transportation. While citing the large number of programs for pre-kindergarten, elementary, and middle school children, the residents noted the lack of recreational and cultural programs for high school students, young adults, and senior citizens.

When asked to identify the most important steps community leaders, working with local officials, could take to stabilize and improve Emerson Park residents proposed the following actions:

1. Hire local unemployed men and women to clean, and otherwise maintain the neighborhood's many unattended vacant lots.

2. Offer contracts to local non-profits, such as the Emerson Park Development Corporation, to seal the neighborhood's many vacant and wide open residential and commercial structures.

3. Recruit members of the recently formed Metro East Enforcement Group of Southern Illinois (MEGSI) to conduct an intensive undercover campaign to challenge local dealers' control of neighborhood streets.

4. Ask nearby municipalities to donate surplus (used) manhole covers to eliminate this threat to pedestrian safety.

5. Work with local churches, fraternal organizations, public schools, and the Neighborhood House to organize low/no-cost recreational and cultural programs for neighborhood teens, young adults, and senior citizens.

In the weeks following our interviews, the class prepared a detailed summary of the 140 resident interviews they had completed. They also carried out an aggressive communications campaign to encourage local stakeholders to attend our final community planning forum where a preliminary draft of the Emerson Park Neighborhood Improvement Plan would be presented. In preparation for this meeting, the students designed individualized meeting invitations for local churches, public schools, civic associations, non-profit organizations, private businesses, and municipal, county, state, and federal agencies with interests in Emerson Park and East St. Louis. They also devised a press release featuring selective highlights from the Emerson Park plan. In addition, they created an attractive flyer that students distributed to residents on a door-to-door basis with the assistance of local leaders. The students also made follow-up telephone calls to local residents and leaders to encourage them to attend this important community meeting.

We pulled into the nearly full Neighborhood House parking lot for the final community planning forum. Carrying copies of the preliminary plan, along with the equipment and materials needed to run the meeting, our students entered the building and warmly greeted many of the residents whom they had gotten to know over the course of project. The students were thrilled to see more than a 125 residents and officials in attendance including Rep. Wyvetter Younge. I thanked her for bringing our team to East St. Louis and Rep. Younge responded saying, "I am pleased to be here this evening. I have been following the university's Emerson Park activities with great interest. Like you, I am looking forward to hearing the students' report and working with EPDC to implement the recommendations residents feel most strongly about. I can tell you this is one of the largest turnouts I have seen for a public meeting of this type in quite some time."

At this point, I turned the meeting over to one of the graduate students who explained that he and his colleagues would be reviewing the highlights of the social history, population profile, physical conditions, and local interview data that they had worked with local residents to collect and analyze. The student encouraged the residents to follow the presentations using the Emerson Park data books they had received upon entering the hall. She said, "This document contains a summary of our research process, major findings, and key planning recommendations. It features wide margins where you can record your questions, criticisms and suggestions. A second graduate student then presented a summary of the revised Emerson Park historical timeline that featured more than fifty events that residents believed shaped their neighborhood's evolution. Residents were extremely pleased to see the dates for the construction of local work places, schools, and churches; formation of the Packinghouse Workers Organizing Committee, and the establishment of the Neighborhood House, among other events, on the timeline.

A third student summarized the results of the class's population and housing trends analyses highlighting Ed's "neighborhood versus the suburbs" comparison that underscored the St. Louis metropolitan region's increasingly uneven pattern of development and concentrated poverty. A fourth student provided a summary of the neighborhood's physical conditions emphasizing Emerson Park's central location, quality building stock, local schools and churches, and large number of vacant lots and abandoned buildings available for redevelopment. A fifth student presented a series of side-by-side tables comparing local leaders and residents' perceptions of the neighborhood's current assets, and problems and future redevelopment opportunities and challenges.

Following these subject-specific reports, a sixth student presented a SWOT analysis summarizing the recurring themes emerging from these data sets. Residents appeared impressed by and, with few exceptions, highly supportive of our team's research findings. During the discussion following these reports, residents complimented the team on the quality of their work while encouraging them to devote additional attention to the improvement of public education, enhanced transportation access to regional employment centers, and strategies to address political corruption.

Pledging to address these weaknesses in their analysis, a seventh student presented a preliminary draft of an overall development goal and specific neighborhood stabilization objectives for stakeholders to consider. He reminded those present that the UIUC team did not formulate these statements while sitting in a computer lab in Champaign-Urbana. Rather, the summary represented their best effort to synthetize local stakeholders' hopes and aspirations for the neighborhood based on more than three months of collaborative research.

Following these comments, the student presented the plan's overall development goal;

"To halt the out-migration of employers, service providers, and residents from the historic Emerson Park neighborhood by means of a comprehensive stabilization plan designed to improve local environmental conditions, public safety, public schools, as well as access to living wage jobs."

The student explained how this goal could be achieved during the next five years by mobilizing Emerson Park's substantial spiritual, financial, physical and social resources to make progress towards accomplishing the following neighborhood stabilization objectives:

1. To dramatically improve environmental conditions through an energetic neighborhood cleanup campaign and stricter enforcement of municipal, state, and federal environmental laws.

2. To enhance residents' perception and experience of public safety through the establishment of neighborhood watch program and community-policing programs.

3. To support local property owners in improving their buildings through the creation of a public/private partnership to assist needy residents in maintaining their properties.

4. To increase the purchase of goods and services provided by local businesses by working with the City of East Louis, School District 159, and area non-profits to initiate a "buy local" program.

5. To investigate transportation alternatives designed to improve current and future residents' access to suburban-based employment opportunities.

Residents responded very positively. They also encouraged our team to add a sixth neighborhood stabilization objective focused on improving public education arguing that good schools were as important as safe streets and living wage jobs to the future health of the community. So a strong statement in support of "promoting excellence in public education" was added to the plan.

The evening's final speaker presented nine immediate (Year 1), intermediate (Years 2-3), and long-term (Years 4-5) projects designed to enable the community to achieve these objectives. Among the specific proposals included in the plan's implementation section were: mobilization of volunteers for a series of neighborhood-wide cleanups; establishment of a neighborhood watch and safety escort service; launch of a Christmas-in-April program to make repairs needed to stabilize the homes of low-income residents; formation of an African dance troupe for neighborhood youth based on East St. Louis' own Katherine Dunham training techniques and choreography; and the creation of a carpooling system to help residents overcome the costs of getting to distant living wage jobs.

Following the last student speaker, I returned to the podium to elicit further resident feedback and to outline the final steps in the planning process. Several residents responded to this invitation by describing the plan as "beautiful," "right on," and "on the money." I replied to these comments by stating that we would be making the changes in the plan that they had suggested by the end of the year, so we could reconvene in January to review the finalized plan and identify available funding to support the most important of its twenty-three neighborhood improvement projects.

The meeting ended on a high note when Bill Kreeb of Neighborhood House, Rev. Jones of the Metro East Area project board, Dr. Kenneth Bonner of the State Community College and Rep. Younge promised to work together to assist the residents in securing the funds needed to implement the plan's major projects. They proposed reconvening on January 15th (Dr. King's birthday) to launch the implementation phase of the planning process—a proposal that received unanimous support from those attending the meeting!

5. IMPLEMENTING THE IMPROVEMENT PLAN

DRIVING BACK TO CAMPUS, the students expressed their satisfaction with the attendance and participation in the final Emerson Park forum and discussed how they planned to organize themselves to complete the revisions suggested by those attending the meeting. Katie Henning then broached the larger and more troubling question, "Who is going to help the residents implement the projects featured in the plan? Research into available funding sources will be needed and grant applications will have to be prepared. Residents are going to require more not less university assistance in the coming months! Do you think the department would consider organizing a spring workshop focused on project design, implementation, and evaluation in East St. Louis?"

A few days later I made an appointment to see Lew Hopkins who informed me that several of my students had already visited to demand a follow-up class. He had completed the paperwork establishing a spring semester "Advanced Neighborhood Planning Workshop" with me as the instructor. During the next ten days the workshop students, Ishaq and I finalized the Emerson Park Neighborhood Improvement Plan and sent it to Davis and her colleagues for final review. We also designed and distributed flyers announcing the newly created Advanced Neighborhood Planning Workshop scheduled for the spring semester. This class quickly filled up, thanks in large part, to the recruitment efforts of our first workshop students

The next community planning forum was scheduled to take place in early February for local stakeholders. Ishaq and I, accompanied by four students, traveled to East St Louis to review the forum agenda with Davis and the Steering Committee. We also spent several hours door-knocking the neighborhood to encourage residents to attend this important meeting.

More than fifty local residents attended the January planning forum. They reviewed the Emerson Park Neighborhood Improvement Plan and identified the three improvement projects they felt should receive immediate attention. After considerable discussion, the residents identified the mobilization of residents and allies for a neighborhood cleanup; formation of a neighborhood crime watch; and a home repair assistance program for low-income residents as their top priorities.

Returning to campus, the class organized themselves into three work groups; to support residents in organizing the neighborhood cleanup by mobilizing both community and campus volunteers; to research best practices in resident-led crime prevention; and to investigate available public and private funding for elder home repairs. Reaching out to service-oriented community and campus-based organizations in Champaign-Urbana the students recruited more than 100 volunteers for the first Emerson Park cleanup scheduled for early April. While investigating innovative approaches to resident-led crime prevention the students discovered the work of Tim Crowe of the National Crime Prevention Institute in Louisville, Kentucky and arranged to interview him. The students' investigation into funding for self-help housing repair and resident-led community development quickly surfaced more than two dozen local, state, and federal government agencies; private foundations; and regional corporations engaged in supporting revitalization efforts within the Greater St. Louis Region.

In February the advanced workshop returned for their second community planning forum to report on the progress being made in identifying community development funding sources, best practices in crime prevention, and sources of volunteers for the spring-cleaning extravaganza. Local residents and leaders decided to contact twenty-seven community development funders, sending a letter i ntroducing the Emerson Park Development Corporation and a bound copy of the recently finalized, 130-page Emerson Park Neighborhood Improvement Plan. It was decided that I would subsequently call each targeted funder to identify those most interested in EPDC's work to schedule a follow-up meeting to explore immediate-term funding opportunities.

Working in small groups, residents generated a list of more than forty community-based crime prevention questions our students should ask the researchers at the National Crime Prevention Institute during our upcoming field trip to this facility. They also came up with a detailed work plan and an equipment and supplies list for the upcoming spring-cleaning extravaganza. Residents decided the spring cleaning should focus on the 9th Street corridor that served as one of the neighborhood's major gateways and the location of more than a dozen badly trashed lots. Davis asked each resident, regardless of their age or infirmity, to participate in the cleanup and to recruit at least three others to do so. She also asked residents to review the list of needed equipment and supplies and commit to providing specific items such as: rakes, shovels, hoes, or boxes of garbage bags.

After returning from East St. Louis, the class completed a highly productive field research trip to the National Crime Prevention Institute at the University of Louisville that included an interview with Dr. Tim Crowe, an internationally recognized expert on the relationship between the built environment and crime. Dr. Crowe gave us access to the Institute's extensive collection of community-based crime prevention materials. Students also conducted a focus group with researchers discussing the effectiveness of alternative resident-led crime prevention programs, including the community policing efforts of William Bratton.

The class subsequently summarized the material they had collected from the Institute and prepared a set of tables describing recent crime trends in East St. Louis based upon the FBI's Uniform Crime Reports. They then scheduled interviews with local residents, institutional leaders, and public officials involved in law enforcement. Meanwhile, Ishaq and I mailed letters and materials to local organizations involved in community development funding in the St. Louis Region.

As the March community planning forum approached the workshop had completed a draft of an *Emerson Park Community Safety Report* featuring a variety of innovative, yet low-cost, proposals for involving local stakeholders in effective crime prevention activities as well as numerous suggestions for enhancing cooperation among local law enforcement organizations, including: the East St. Louis Police Department (ESLPD), and the Metro East

Enforcement Group for Southern Illinois (MEGSI). Our students, along with Bruce Sylvester, the graduate research assistant assigned to our workshop, recruited nearly 100 campus and community volunteers for our first Emerson Park cleanup. Among these volunteers were members of Lambda Alpha Fraternity, Tri-Delta Sorority, Hillel Association, Arab Student League, as well as the St. John Lutheran Church's Boy Scout troop. Our students also managed to recruit Lew Hopkins, the head of the Department of Urban and Regional Planning to participate in the event.

While the class was making impressive progress Ishaq and I had run into a stonewall on the community development funding front. A dozen or so leaders of local community development agencies had agreed to meet with us regarding the Emerson Park Neighborhood Improvement Plan. They congratulated us for undertaking a project in such a challenging environment, complimented our team on the high level of citizen participation we had achieved, and praised our workshop for the quality of our plan, but not a single professional we met with was willing to recommend or commit funding for any of the projects, contained in our plan. Quoting one senior planning official from the region, "My board would run me out of town if I brought your plan to them for funding. There is a near universal belief among our board that there is little, if anything, that can be done to turn East St. Louis around." Shortly after returning from the last of these funders' meetings, I shared my mounting frustration over our inability to interest funders in EPDC's work with Kieran Donaghy, my former Cornell classmate and then UIUC colleague, who had originally encouraged me to work in East St. Louis. With a wry smile, Kieran responded by saying, "For most professionals, the notion of planning in East St. Louis is like visiting the morgue to determine the health of the cadavers. You go once to pronounce them dead and to inform their loved ones, so they can move on."

Before the March community planning forum, we carried out our typical pre-meeting outreach, including a combined resident and institutional mailing, church announcements, press releases, follow-up phone calls, and door knocking. Approximately sixty-five local stakeholders attended. The community's response to the preliminary draft of the Emerson Park community safety plan was very positive. Aware of the serious manpower, equipment, and corruption challenges facing the East St. Louis Police Department, residents were pleased to learn about the many resident-led public safety initiatives they could pursue, independent of local law enforcement, to reduce crime in their neighborhood. They seemed particularly interested in the plan's fire and security survey proposals that focused on the training of EPDC leaders by local law enforcement, fire safety, and industrial security experts to perform inspections of residential, commercial, and non-profit properties to identify low-cost improvements designed to reduce the risk of household/ business accidents, fires, and burglaries. They were also excited by the group buying proposal designed to enable local residents, business, and institutions to secure better prices for common fire safety and security equipment, such as fire extinguishers, smoke alarms, motion sensor lighting, and high quality locks by combining their purchasing power in order to negotiate discounts with regional and national home improvement chains, such as Lowe's and Home Depot.

The crime watch proposal was purposely described in general terms out of a concern that some of those attending might, in fact, be involved in the neighborhood's increasingly active and violent illegal drug trade. On the advice of Bruce Reppert, the First Assistant U.S. Attorney for the Southern District of Illinois, EPDC's leaders and our students decided to begin quietly building a network of neighborhood crime reporters starting with EPDC's leaders and most active members who were known to be uninvolved in this lucrative activity. In the subsequent weeks and months, we slowly established a neighborhood-wide network of well-trained crime reporters using a snowballing technique that enabled EPDC to generate hundreds of highly accurate crime reports. These helped MEGSI to disrupt and disable this market by arresting dozens of street-level dealers in the fall of 1991 and the spring of 1992, dramatically reducing the level of street crime within the neighborhood.

Following the unanimous endorsement of the Emerson Park Public Safety Plan by the community, Davis and our students reported on the impressive progress that had been made organizing the upcoming cleanup. More than 180 community and campus volunteers were committed to participate. Equipment and supplies had been gathered, and participants were to be fed through the combined efforts of Catholic Urban Programs, Lessie Bates Davis Neighborhood House and EPDC volunteers. Both Rep. Wyvetter Younge and Mayor Carl Officer had promised to participate.

We then moved onto the last item on our agenda—the status of our external fundraising campaign, I explained how we had sent letters introducing EPDC's list of past and planned revitalization efforts, along with copies of our recently completed plan, to approximately two dozen funders of local economic and community development projects within the St. Louis Region. I then described how Ishaq and I had subsequently called the directors of these organizations to request one-on-one meetings to explore their interest in funding the plan's initiatives. I finished my report by telling the residents that we had failed to identify a single regional funder willing to invest in their neighborhood in spite of the quality of the plan, high level of local stakeholder support, and strong UIUC endorsement. Sensing both my embarrassment and frustration, Ceola Davis got up, gave me a hug, and said, "Ken, what did you expect - a check? We are simply going to have to implement our plan with the resources at hand!" Sensing my confusion, she asked those in the room to, "Raise your hand if you are going to be joining us for next month's spring-cleaning extravaganza! Raise your other hand if you are going to be bringing others to help, equipment or supplies to use, or food for the troops!" Looking around the room, nearly every resident and student had one or both of their hands in the air, Davis turned to me and said, "How can we fail? Others will help us implement our plan. Remember the *Field of Dreams*—if you build it, they will come! You just gotta have a little faith!"

Driving back to campus, I was struck by the privilege that my reaction to our failed fundraising efforts had reflected. As a middle-class, Ivy-League educated, white professional, I had never experienced the kind of universal rejection from those in power as I had when trying to assist EPDC in securing support for their plan. My experiences coming from a relatively well-resourced and politically connected New York City family had led me to believe that a carefully pursued planning process that generated a high-quality plan would, in most cases, be supported by local officials. The experiences of Davis and her neighbors, on the other hand, caused them to have serious doubts regarding the willingness of local elites to invest in severely distressed communities such as Emerson Park. Where my students and I, given our racial and class identities, expected support for the Emerson Park Neighborhood Improvement Plan from "jump street"—our community partners realized that such support would only come through repeated demonstrations of local economic and community development success supported by ongoing community outreach, organizing, and popular struggle.

Several weeks after this meeting, the workshop students accompanied by three busloads of volunteers traveled to Emerson Park for the inaugural spring-cleaning extravaganza along the 9th street corridor. At the Neighborhood House, the volunteers were greeted by the smell of St. Louis BBQ and applause from seventy residents Davis had recruited. As students removed the equipment, they planned to use for the cleanup from Prof. Hopkins' van, we paused for a short prayer and a few remarks by Rep. Young who told the volunteers that the day's cleanup represented much more than the removal of illegally dumped trash from the neighborhood. According to Rep. Younge, "You are participating in a historic and unprecedented effort by residents of Illinois' poorest African-American community to reclaim their neighborhood and city. So, let's get to work!"

Community and campus volunteers participating in the Emerson Park spring cleanup extravaganza preparing to leave campus (Photo by K. Reardon).

For the next six hours, teams cleared household trash, building debris and discarded auto parts and tires from a dozen vacant lots and the right-of-way along a four-block stretch of 9th Street. The household trash and demolition debris were neatly stacked against the curbs on both sides of the street. The used automobile and truck tires were rolled to a centrally located vacant lot –a task complicated by the stagnant water and mosquitos often found inside the tires.

While helping a group of East St. Louis and UIUC volunteers shovel household trash from a lot into large trash bags, Richard Suttle leaned over and said, "Well Dr. Reardon, you and your students have just distinguished yourselves from 99% of the "do-gooders" who've come to East St. Louis. You have actually gotten off your rear ends to do a messy, yet, critical job—removing hazards that threatened our children and elders' health and well-being. Congratulations!"

While I was initially irritated, by Suttle's remarks, I later came to understand his frustration with the army of university-trained planners and designers that regularly came to East St. Louis offering urban revitalization proposals without so much as lifting a finger to support any of the scores of resident-led stabilization and redevelopment efforts already underway.

The 9th street corridor prior to EPDC/ESLARP's Clean up (Photo by K. Reardon)

During the remainder of the day, teams of community and university volunteers gathered more than 900 bags of household trash and building debris. As the volunteers leaned into the work, several of the area's older residents brought them cold water and sweet tea. Teens and young adults living in the bungalows along 9th street also came out to join the effort. A block-long stretch of 9th street was lined with bulging trash bags prompting volunteers to ask when the trucks would be arriving. When Davis was asked about the trucks, she just smiled.

As we wrapped up our work and prepared to head home, a KMOV-TV News van and reporter appeared, prompted by a call from Rep. Younge who explained to the reporter how residents threatened by years of illegal dumping had decided, without the support of local officials, to take steps to restore the health of their neighborhood. She then proceeded to describe how residents unable to get the area's absentee property owners or the City of East St. Louis to address this problem had, with the support of University of Illinois volunteers, entered private property to remove accumulations of trash and debris to protect the public health. At Neighborhood House the volunteers washed, ate, and watched KMOV's evening news that included the following headline—*Community Residents Break Law to Save East St. Louis Neighborhood.* The volunteers cheered as the reporter explained how local residents and their university allies had gone on to privately and municipally-owned properties, without permission, to address a growing public health threat, i.e. illegal dumping.

During the long trip back to campus, Ishaq, Bruce Sylvester, and I thanked the students for making the trip, asking them to share a highlight of their day with those travelling on their bus. Without exception, the students expressed their delight with how much had been accomplished, the large number of residents contributing to the effort, and the warm welcome they had received from the community. They also shared their shock over seeing such devastation in an Illinois city. Commenting on the large number of remaining illegal dump sites, several students asked when the next community cleanup would be and how they could get involved in the next neighborhood planning workshop they had heard so much about.

Several days after our trip, Ceola Davis called to share three exciting developments with us. St. Clair County officials who had watched the KMOV News story had quickly dispatched trucks to remove the trash bags and discarded tires that had been collected along 9th street. Also, hearing about the cleanup at church, several long-time residents had stopped by the Neighborhood House to join EPDC. According to Davis, they liked that fact that it was a group that "Not only talked the talk, but walked the walk!" Finally, Bill Kreeb, of the Neighborhood House received a significant donation from an area foundation to support the residents' ongoing environmental stewardship activities.

Encouraged by these developments, Davis worked with EPDC over the summer to organize several additional cleanup days, removing household trash and building debris from dozens of nearby lots. These efforts soon came to the attention of the commanding officer of the nearby Illinois National Guard Armory who mobilized his men and their heavy equipment to support the Emerson Park cleanup as a part of their ongoing disaster response and resiliency training programs. At the same time, Bruce Reppert of the U.S. Attorney's office pursued indictments against the trash haulers whose refuse was mysteriously appearing in East St. Louis' poorest neighborhoods. A direct result of these efforts was a dramatic reduction in the level of illegal dumping taking place in East St. Louis and a multi-million-dollar settlement that provided local governments with much-needed support for environmental enforcement and cleanup activities. These developments, reinforced by the selection of Emerson Park Neighborhood Improvement Plan as the Best Student Project of 1991 by the American Institute of Certified Planners, generated a great deal of excitement regarding the project among community residents as well as UIUC students and faculty.

6. THE PROGRAM FOR MINORITY STUDENTS IN LANSDOWNE

AS THE SUMMER OF 1991 approached, Ishaq and I briefed R. Alan Forester, Director of the School of Architecture, Vince Bellafiore, head of the Department of Landscape Architecture, and Lew Hopkins on the successes and failures of our past year's activities in East St. Louis. Among the issues we discussed were the importance of continuing our Emerson Park efforts until they could be sustained by local institutions; the need to pursue a more interdisciplinary approach to our work by integrating architecture and landscape architecture students and faculty into the effort; and, finally, using the project to recruit minority students into UIUC's architecture, landscape architecture, and urban planning programs where they were significantly underrepresented.

We decided to organize an eight-week summer program to introduce African-American, Latino, Asian, and Native American undergraduates to opportunities available within the fields of architecture, landscape architecture, and urban and regional planning. A secondary objective of this program was to encourage community-oriented undergraduate students of color to consider pursuing planning and design degrees at UIUC. We sought to achieve these two goals by involving ten to twenty undergraduate students of color from schools throughout the U.S. in an interdisciplinary planning workshop designed to produce a comprehensive revitalization plan for a second East St. Louis neighborhood.

Excited by the prospects of initiating our first interdisciplinary planning effort in East St. Louis, Professors Forester and Bellafiore recruited a studio instructor from their respective programs to work with me on a minority summer program in architecture, landscape, and urban and regional planning. Michael Andrejasich, an Associate Professor of Architecture, and Brian Orland, a Professor in Landscape Architecture, came to speak with me about the proposed summer program. In sharing our personal histories, we discovered

Students and faculty participants in the 1991 summer program in architecture, landscape architecture, and planning for minority students (Photo by ESLARP Staff)

that each of us had grown up in religious households where the social gospel was a common topic of conversation and had received our professional degrees from programs deeply involved in community-based research, planning, and design.

Michael, Brian, and I established the structure of the curriculum and discussed how we might recruit additional faculty to participate in the summer program in hopes of encouraging their ongoing participation in resident-led change efforts in East St. Louis. We ultimately succeeded in recruiting nine faculty members to serve as part-time instructors for the summer program. Among these were Ernie Clay, Jeff Poss, and Kevin Hinders from Architecture; Terry Harkness, Gary Kessler, and Carol Emmerling-DiNovo from Landscape Architecture; and Kieran Donaghy, Len Heumann, and Rob Olshansky from the Urban and Regional Planning department.

While these individuals worked together to create compelling introductions to their professions for our prospective summer school students, I focused on recruiting minority students for the program and identifying an East St. Louis neighborhood whose residents were interested in partnering with UIUC on the development of a comprehensive stabilization plan. I reached out via mailings and personal contacts to UIUC undergraduate programs with significant minority enrollments, to Historically Black Colleges and Universities (HBCUs), and to a number of urban serving universities with high minority enrollments. Through these activities, I recruited fifteen students for UIUC's inaugural summer program for minority students in architecture, landscape architecture, and urban and regional planning. Among the campuses where we successfully recruited students were UIUC, the University of Illinois at Chicago, Hunter College, Alabama A & M, and Texas A & M.

Following a series of conversations with EPDC's leaders, UIUC extension staff, and Rep. Younge we selected the Lansdowne neighborhood, located immediately southeast of Emerson Park, to launch our second neighborhood planning effort. Residents of this working-class community had been carefully monitoring our Emerson Park activities and had recently asked Rev. Jones, whose church was located in this neighborhood, to encourage the university to extend their planning efforts to their neighborhood. Among the issues confronting their community were the long-term decline of Jones Park, the city's largest park located in the heart of the neighborhood; a dramatic shift from homeownership to absentee property ownership; and the proposed construction of the Jackie Joyner-Kersee Youth Recreation and Cultural Center at a site immediately adjacent to Jones Park.

The nine UIUC faculty participating in our first summer program devoted three weeks to providing basic instruction on the history, theory, and methods of their respective disciplines to our students. One of the most exciting aspects of the program was the attendance and active involvement of participating architecture, landscape architecture, and urban planning faculty in all three of these discipline-specific introductions. For the majority of faculty trained in rigidly "siloed" architectural schools and urban planning institutes, this was the first time in their academic careers they had the opportunity to significantly enrich their knowledge of the other design professions.

Following three weeks of classroom-based instruction, the summer school students and faculty shifted their attention to the collection and analysis of primary and secondary data on historic trends, existing conditions, and future revitalization options needed to prepare a stabilization plan for the Lansdowne community. The involvement of architecture and landscape architecture faculty in the data collection and analysis phase of the planning process produced a number of improvements in the planning methodology we had been using in East St. Louis. The landscape architecture faculty showed students how historic maps, generated by various local, state, and federal agencies could be used to reveal the process by which the land's natural features had shaped the Lansdowne neighborhood's physical development and land uses.

The landscape architecture faculty also introduced the use of disposable cameras as a participatory planning tool. They encouraged us to invite residents to use these cameras to document their neighborhood's most significant assets, challenges, and untapped resources. This highly accessible activity gave more than fifty Lansdowne residents an important new role during the research phase of the planning process. This simple tool also helped students and faculty involved in the Lansdowne planning process generate a fine-grained existing conditions map while giving residents an enhanced sense of ownership over the planning process.

Meanwhile, the architecture faculty used their experience analyzing the structural integrity and historical significance of residential, commercial, industrial, and civic buildings and urban infrastructure to significantly improve the land use, building conditions, and site maintenance and the urban infrastructure surveys we had used in Emerson Park. They also utilized their mastery of the computer's multi-media functions to teach students how to attach photographic images and physical conditions notes to each property we surveyed, allowing them to subsequently share, in real time, detailed information regarding every property during classes and community meetings. This interactive feature of the neighborhood maps significantly enhanced the quality of the policy and planning discussions that took place during our subsequent community meetings.

Following four weeks of intense library, internet, and field-based data collection and analysis, the summer school students and faculty shifted their attention to the production of a high-quality neighborhood plan that was subsequently presented to approximately fifty residents and community leaders at a meeting of the Lansdowne Area Neighborhood Development Organization (LANDO) held at Rev. Jones' church. A notable difference between the audience that had gathered to hear the presentation of the preliminary drafts of the Emerson Park and Lansdowne plans was the attendance of a significant number of important public and private sector leaders at the latter forum. Among those present at the Lansdowne meeting was the president of the city's largest bank, a senior program officer from the East St. Louis Community Foundation, a board member from the Jackie Joiner-Kersee Foundation, president of the board of trustees of State Community College, staff from the Katherine Dunham Centers for Art and Humanities, officials from the East St. Louis Mayor and City Manager's offices, and delegates from Rep. Younge's office, and State Senator Kenneth Hall's office. Throughout the meeting, these officials asked our summer school students detailed questions regarding the policies, programs, and projects they were recommending that they handled with considerable skill.

Our students and faculty were delighted at the end of the meeting when representatives of the Mayor's office encouraged our team to work with LANDO on a proposal to the city's CDBG program to fund several of the plan's most important physical improvement projects. Encouraged by the positive response the Lansdowne Neighborhood Improvement Plan had received from local residents, institutional leaders, and municipal officials, Carla Spradlin, a UIUC graduate planning student, subsequently offered to prepare a five-year CDBG application to the city as her master of city and regional planning capstone project.

UIUC faculty was excited by the success of the summer school as an interdisciplinary professional education, minority recruitment, and community development assistance initiative. The majority of the participating students and faculty viewed the program as a unique and very valuable opportunity to deepen their planning and design skills as part of an interdisciplinary team of urban professionals. The number of undergraduate students from UIUC and other participating schools that subsequently decided to pursue graduate studies in architecture, landscape architecture, and urban and regional planning at UIUC thrilled the faculty. The decision by a majority of the UIUC students and faculty who had participated in

Summer school students, led by Howard Johnson from Alabama A&M., present their Lansdowne Neighborhood Improvement Plan (Photo by K. Reardon).

the summer program to continue their involvement in East St. Louis during the 1991–1992 academic year represented another extremely positive outcome. Finally, the growing support that the university's East St. Louis outreach project received from the city's newly elected leaders, especially Mayor Gordon Bush, a highly respected career army officer, following the summer school program was deeply gratifying. Aware of the city's limited ability to pursue discretionary state and federal grants for infrastructure, housing, and economic development without a fully-staffed planning office, Mayor Bush and his colleagues, believed the university's East St. Louis initiative could assist them in generating high-quality plans and external funding proposals to address the city's most critical needs.

As the summer program came to an end, the faculty who had been most deeply involved in the Lansdowne planning process, including Michael Andrejasich, Brian Orland, Gary Kessler, and I met to discuss the future of the university's East St. Louis effort. All of us believed the interdisciplinary approach to urban problem solving reflected in our Lansdowne planning effort could significantly enhance the quality of our college's professional education programs. At the time, increasing numbers of towns and cities in the U.S. and abroad were seeking planning and design services from consulting firms that approached their work from an interdisciplinary perspective—a type of practice that few planning and design schools prepared their students to lead. The group also felt the quality of university's applied research, city plans, and urban designs in East St. Louis would be significantly improved if our students pursued this work with the support of interdisciplinary teams of experienced faculty rather than a single professor. In addition, the faculty believed the long-term sustainability and effectiveness of the university's East St. Louis engaged scholarship activities required a stronger base of institutional support and significant external funding.

Based upon this discussion, we developed a proposal for re-organizing the university's East St. Louis outreach efforts that we presented to Professors Forester, Bellafiore, and Hopkins and Dean Katherine Martin that featured the following elements.

1. Continue to develop the university's East St. Louis project as an interdisciplinary community planning, design and development initiative by combining the East St. Louis funds currently being provided to support individual faculty efforts in the architecture, landscape architecture, and urban and regional planning units into a college-wide resource to support interdisciplinary field-based education, applied research, and community outreach efforts in the city.

2. Support studio-based projects undertaken by students and faculty in architecture, landscape architecture, and urban and regional planning by providing these, and potentially other academic units, with dedicated funding for graduate research assistants, travel support, and program expenses for fall planning-focused studios and spring project implementation-focused studios for upper level undergraduate and first-year graduate students in each of these units while encouraging as much collaborative work among the units as possible.

3. Allocate a recurring amount of funding to establish a project website to: document past, current, and proposed work; provide participating students and faculty with access to previously completed East St. Louis research; assist in the coordination of collaborative activities undertaken by the

participating academic units; offer East St. Louis residents, professionals, and officials access to UIUC-generated East St. Louis scholarship; promote the dissemination of East St. Louis-generated innovations among interested professionals and scholars throughout the globe; provide a forum for popular, professional, and scholarly organizations to discuss the thrills, spills, and chills of resident-led planning, design, and development in severely distressed communities, such as East St. Louis; and, make the extraordinary contributions to democratic planning and sustainable development being made by resident-led planning, development, and design organizations in East St. Louis more visible to other citizen groups, professional organizations, policy-making institutions, and external funders.

4. Ensure greater accountability to the community by institutionalizing a majority resident policy-making body while initiating a participatory formative evaluation process for the project.

Professors Forester, Bellafiore, Hopkins, and Martin enthusiastically supported these proposals, promising to secure the approval of UIUC's Provost and President as well as the support of Rep. Younge. As they did so, they encouraged the summer school faculty who appeared most interested in continuing their involvement in the program to form a faculty advisory committee to provide interim direction to the project until an appropriate community/university governance structure, involving local residents, institutional leaders, and elected officials, could be established. Within a few days of this meeting, the Dean's office informed us that UIUC's Provost and President's Office, as well as the representative, supported our reorganization plan.

Inspired by the news, Michael, Brian, and I invited several of the College of Fine and Applied Arts faculty to join a newly organized faculty advisory committee. We were further energized when Kevin Hinders and Bob Selby from architecture, Gary Kessler and Carol Emmerling-DiNovo from landscape architecture, and Kieran Donaghy and Varkki George Pallathucheril from urban planning decided to join the faculty advisory committee which began meeting on a weekly basis.

Finally, we decided to change the project's name from University Extension and Minority Access Project (UEMAP) to the East St. Louis Action Research Project (ESLARP) to highlight the initiative's focus on East St. Louis, our use of a highly participatory approach to community planning, and our commitment to translating research into action to enhance the quality of life for those with the fewest resources and opportunities.

7. THE PARTNERSHIP IN WINSTANLEY/ INDUSTRIAL PARK

IN THE SUMMER OF 1991, we received a call from Rev. Gary Wilson, pastor of the Wesley Bethel United Methodist Church. He asked us to work with his congregation and neighbors to prepare a comprehensive stabilization plan for Winstanley/Industrial Park similar to the ones we had recently completed for the Emerson Park and Lansdowne neighborhoods. During the call, Rev. Wilson explained how a number of well-known community leaders had recently come together—inspired by the work of the Emerson Park Development Corporation (EPDC)—to establish their own community development corporation, the Winstanley Industrial Park Neighborhood Organization (WIPNO) to address the underlying causes of their neighborhood's decline.

After discussing the call with the faculty advisory committee, I travelled to East St. Louis to meet Rev. Wilson whose church was located directly across the street from the Orr-Weathers Housing Complex—the city's largest public housing complex. Rev. Wilson began the meeting with a short history of his neighborhood highlighting the important leadership role local churches and minority businesses had played in fighting for the community. He then discussed his desire to use UIUC's participatory planning process to build a strong base of support for a revitalization strategy focused on job generation, housing development, crime prevention, youth services, and food security.

Following our meeting, Rev. Wilson took me on a neighborhood tour that included several areas of beautifully maintained single-family homes, The Orr-Weathers Housing Complex, a corridor of recently-shuttered industrial businesses, numerous churches and social service agencies and several vital local businesses. Upon my return to campus, I shared the results of my Winstanley/Industry Park meeting and tour with the committee encouraging them to join me for a follow-up meeting with Rev. Wilson and representatives of the WIPNO to explore the possibility of making their neighborhood the focus of our East St. Louis activities during the 1991–1992 academic year.

The following week, Professors Michael Andrejasich, Brian Orland and Bob Selby accompanied me to East St. Louis to meet with WIPNO's leaders. Among those we met with were Carol Perry, a former Monsanto salesperson and marketing executive; James Perry, a recently-retired East St. Louis fireman and local building contractor; Delores Turnbaugh, a former public school teacher; Rev. Herman Watson, the newly-appointed pastor of the Mt. Sinai Missionary Baptist Church; Deacon Earl Dobbins Jr., an elder from Rev. Watson's congregation; and Rev. Wilson, our original Winstanley/Industry Park contact.

While these individuals appreciated the value of comprehensive neighborhood planning, they were keenly aware of the cynical view most Winstanley/Industry Park residents had of city planning and urban revitalization. In discussing strategies for overcoming these barriers, Carol Perry asked if it might be possible to undertake our planning in a slightly different manner than we had in Emerson Park and Lansdowne. "Could we engage in a bit of parallel processing? Could we aggressively pursue the traditional planning process while simultaneously carrying out a series of modest but highly visible improvement projects to convince skeptics that we are committed to taking meaningful action for change?" asked Perry.

I was concerned about our ability to simultaneously manage a labor-intensive planning process and a series of small-scale but demanding, improvement projects. But the leaders strongly supported Carol Perry's "ready, fire, aim" approach, and quickly generated an impressive list of projects they felt could stimulate broad-based resident interest in the Winstanley/Industry Park planning process. Among this list of projects were:

1. Clean-up of trash-strewn lots;

2. Board-up of structurally sound and architecturally significant abandoned buildings;

3. Installation of "Welcome to Industry/Park" entranceway signs;

4. Expansion of the heavily used St. Clair County Head Start playground at the Wesley Bethel United Methodist Church;

5. Construction of a vest pocket park in northeastern Winstanley/Industry; and,

6. Exterior repairs to the homes of low-income seniors and persons with disabilities.

We agreed that in addition to having my neighborhood planning workshop focus on producing a comprehensive stabilization plan for the neighborhood, we would have our architecture and landscape architecture studios simultaneously undertake the research needed to execute a series of small-scale improvement projects. We also suggested extending the neighborhood planning process from one to two semesters in order to have the time needed to carryout this more complex work program.

During our return trip to campus, Michael, Brian, Bob and I discussed the kinds of "hands on" projects to undertake. We agreed that the Head Start playground project—based upon the number of children and families it served— would have the greatest impact on the neighborhood. We then discussed the significant visual impact that landscape projects such as this could have on community perceptions of existing conditions as well as future development possibilities. Brian and Michael highlighted the relatively low cost/high impact and modest skill requirements of open space improvement projects such as this.

Brian, Michael and Bob, who were architects with considerable construction experience, also saw significant benefit in making modest exterior repairs to residential structures that might otherwise be at risk of abandonment. They believed that a small number of exterior home repairs undertaken throughout the neighborhood could positively impact residents' perceptions of the area's future. But my colleagues identified three issues that would have to be addressed. First, they were concerned that local design professionals (i.e. architects and landscape architects) might view these UIUC-sponsored design/build projects as "unfair" (i.e. publicly subsidized) competition. Second, given the city's long history of cronyism related to publicly supported redevelopment projects, they were nervous about the process by which families would be selected for this program. Third, they were anxious about possible student accidents and injuries and related liability issues if ESLARP got involved in major design/build projects.

In the weeks following this meeting, Andrejasich contacted the St. Louis Metro chapter of the American Institute of Architects regarding the issue of unfair university competition with licensed professionals in the region. The local AIA leadership indicated they had no problem with our proposed home improvement projects, which they viewed as emergency stabilization efforts. However, in the event these and other university-supported revitalization stimulated new public and private investment they said they would expect the resulting planning and design work to be done by area professionals in good standing with their respective professional associations. After assuring the local AIA Chapter of our full support for their position, they wished us success with our grassroots revitalization campaign in East St. Louis. Having resolved this issue, we subsequently contacted UIUC's Office of Risk Management regarding our potential involvement in a variety of landscape installation and building-focused "design/build" projects in East St. Louis.

Representatives of this office were extremely helpful! During several conversations, we learned that UIUC was self-insured. While this status gave students, faculty, and staff more flexibility in designing "insurable" research, teaching, and outreach programs; it also required university staff to exercise considerable care in structuring program activities, selecting research/teaching/ learning venues, identifying partners, choosing equipment, and training and supervising students as they pursued field-based research activities. Ultimately, the office agreed to cover our proposed experiential learning activities provided we followed several basic procedures, including: requiring pre-field orientation for all participants; refraining from using fifteen-passenger vans for travel; maintaining reasonable student/faculty ratios; offering basic tool safety instruction; requiring students to wear appropriate safety gear and providing close supervision of students by faculty and graduate research assistants with construction experience and tool safety knowledge.

With these issues resolved, we spoke to Rev. Wilson, Rev. Watson, and Elder Dobbins regarding the process by which we would select and prioritize residential homes to be repaired. They suggested we limit our initial improvement activities to the homes of senior citizens, persons with disabilities, and low-income Veterans. They also recommended using area churches, social service agencies, and public schools to elicit requests for assistance. Finally, they volunteered to screen and select families with the greatest shelter needs for this assistance.

Having successfully addressed our major design/build concerns, Professors Andrejasich, Orland, and Selby began working with several architecture and landscape architecture students with building construction and landscape installation knowledge and skills to identify the training, equipment, supplies, permits, logistical support, and funding needed to successfully execute the kinds of physical improvement projects that resident leaders had identified, specifically, the Head Start playground expansion and exterior home improvement projects.

With the 1991 fall semester just weeks away, we convened a second meeting with WIPNO's leaders to review our preliminary scope of services and timetable for completing the Winstanley/Industry Park Neighborhood Improvement Plan. We agreed to focus our fall planning workshop on the collection and analysis of the data required to produce a high quality neighborhood stabilization plan. We further agreed to have our spring planning workshop concentrate on producing the prescriptive portion of the plan while our architecture and landscape architecture colleagues focused on the expansion of the St. Clair County Head Start playground and the exterior scraping, spackling, priming, and painting of the home of a revered neighborhood elder.

Before ending this meeting, we outlined our basic outreach and media strategy to inform local stakeholders about WIPNO, the upcoming neighborhood planning process, and the planned community improvement projects. As we did in Emerson Park and Lansdowne, we proposed press releases, letters to area institutional leaders, flyers sent home with neighborhood school children, storefront posters, as well as individualized hand-delivered resident letters. WINPO's leaders also suggested we send students to the Sunday services of local religious congregations to introduce ourselves and extend personal invitations to these groups to join the planning process.

Believing church visits to be an excellent idea but concerned about mandating attendance at religious services for students at a public university, we somewhat nervously added this activity to our first Winstanley/Industry Park orientation and outreach weekend. Upon returning to campus, Michael, Brian, Bob and I organized our students to research Winstanley/Industry Park's social history; document it's recent population, economic, and housing trends using U.S. Census data; investigate local property ownership and assessed value data using the Assessor's office database; prepare materials needed to execute our community media and outreach strategies; and develop preliminary plans for several small-scale neighborhood improvement projects.

An early "scrape-up, paint-up" project carried out by UIUC students during one of ESLARP's first "East St. Louis Work Weekends" (Photo by K. Reardon).

We also informed the students in our studios that we would be travelling to East St. Louis in two weeks to meet with our new community partner, WIPNO's executive committee, to tour the neighborhood, inspect the sites of our initial improvement projects, and to put up posters at local stores, schools, and agencies, and visit area churches to encourage them to become actively involved in the neighborhood planning process. While the students appeared to be universally excited about the upcoming field trip, they were decidedly unenthusiastic about the proposed church visits. One student stated, "My parents have been unable to get me to go to church! How can the U of I, a state institution, require me to participate in Sunday services?"

Sensitive to this student's concerns and unsure of my right, as an untenured professor, to mandate church attendance, I responded in the following manner, "We are not asking you to attend church services in hopes of saving your souls. Let's face it, most of us don't have what it takes to be even marginal Baptists. We are asking you to attend church services as a sign of our respect for the community's values and traditions and because this is the single most important institution within the African-American community. You can't pursue participatory planning and design without engaging members of the local community. In the case of Winstanley/Industry Park and most other African-American communities, the black church is the most important democratic space within the community—a place where people come to share their deepest hopes, desires, and disappointments with their neighbors."

The following week a group of approximately twenty-five architecture, landscape architecture, and urban and regional planning students travelled to East St. Louis for a two-day orientation. On Friday, the group held a productive meeting with WIPNO's executive committee followed by a tour of the neighborhood led by Rev. Wilson and Carol Perry. On Saturday, we completed an initial community assets inventory of the study area by walking the neighborhood noting the locations of important natural features, historic sites and structures, churches, social service agencies, educational institutions, local businesses, and other community resources. After this, one team visited the St. Clair County Head Start playground to produce "as built" drawings of the current facilities and to discuss possible site improvements with Rev. Wilson and the Head Start's lead teacher/site manager. A second group visited the retail businesses, commercial offices, human service organizations, and religious institutions located along Dr. Martin Luther King Jr. Boulevard (the neighborhood's major commercial corridor) to inform them of the Winstanley/Industry Park neighborhood planning process and to request permission to post public service announcements regarding this effort on their premises. The third group, fortified by a handful of WIPNO members, canvassed the neighborhood to inform residents about the soon-to-be-launched planning process encouraging them to become actively involved in this process. While all of the students encountered a handful of skeptical local stakeholders who were uninterested in WIPNO's efforts; the majority of the students made contact with a much larger number of individuals who were excited to hear about this new resident-led planning process and looked forward to attending WIPNO's inaugural community planning forum scheduled to take place in two weeks.

The following morning, we met in the motel lobby to assign students to visit six of the neighborhood's largest religious congregations. Rev. Wilson had called each of the pastors to inform them that we would be visiting their churches to formally invite them to participate in the planning process. I advised students that if they were allowed to make an announcement, they should emphasize our belief that the creation of an effective community stabilization plan would be impossible without the prophetic voice of the local faith community. I also encouraged them, regardless of their own faith traditions, to carefully observe what was going on during the service and, to the extent they felt comfortable, to actively participate in the liturgy. In attending services that morning, I told the students they would be joining a very small percentage of planning and design professionals working in communities of color that had taken the time to attend black church services to demonstrate their respect for this community's history and culture and to acquire an understanding of how leaders of this important community institution view existing community conditions and future development possibilities.

I then assigned the students to specific congregations and proceeded to drive a vanload to three local congregations. Approaching my last drop-off at the Second Avenue Baptist Church on MLK Blvd, I noticed four well-dressed men wearing white gloves who were serving as greeters. I also heard the church choir supported by the congregation. Pulling up to the curb, I invited the last three students in the van to remember my earlier instructions and to enjoy the service. At that point, Howard Johnson, one of our former summer program students who had subsequently enrolled in our planning program, observed how nervous his two classmates, who were Japanese exchange students, appeared to be. Turning to me he asked, "Professor Reardon, you will be joining us, won't you?" Realizing the spirited liturgy of this Black evangelical church might be a shock for two Buddhists whose previous religious observances were most likely dominated by quiet meditation, I made a last-minute decision to attend church with my students. As we got out of the van, one of the greeters immediately welcomed us saying. "You must be our friends from the University of Illinois." As we entered the church, the greeter informed an usher that we were the congregation's special guests. Smiling, the usher escorted us to our seats near the front of the congregation.

Midway through the service, I heard the pastor announce our presence to the congregation whose members gave us an enthusiastic round of applause. Asking us to stand, the pastor asked us to share our names and "home churches" with the congregants, which we did. He then asked me to explain our reason for visiting his church on that day. I proceeded to thank the pastor, the elders, and the church members for welcoming us to their service. I then explained how neighborhood leaders had recently come together to form a group, called the Winstanley/Industry Park Neighborhood Organization, to restore the health and vitality of this historic African-American community. I then described how UIUC was actively supporting this effort by preparing a comprehensive stabilization plan for the community. I finished my remarks by inviting their church to join this important community transformation effort. Responding with a loud "Amen," the pastor asked the congregation to raise their hands in our direction as he called on God to bless our efforts.

When the service ended, members approached us to introduce themselves, invite us to their social hour, and ask the date and location of WIPNO's next meeting. After spending a half-hour in the church basement meeting additional members of the congregation, we returned to the van where the students immediately burst into laughter. Howard began the conversation by stating, "Hey, I am a Baptist but I have never experienced a service like this before. My family would describe this as a 'Holy Ghost' church where people are guided by the spirit rather than theology or tradition." The beauty of the spirituals, along with the passion of the congregation, impressed our Japanese students. Both said they couldn't wait to tell their parents about being "saved" in East St. Louis. Gathering for a late lunch at a nearby restaurant, the students excitedly exchanged stories regarding their black church experiences. After hearing them describe the transformative effect of attending local services, I kidded them by saying; "I don't think the Catholic, Presbyterian, or Lutheran churches would last a year, if their members had the opportunity to experience a black church service in East St. Louis." One of the students then said, "You drive through the neighborhood and its physical appearance gives you the sense of a community in deep trouble; you then go to church where you experience the residents' extraordinary vision, passion, and commitment which gives you a completely different sense of the neighborhood and its possibilities." Another student encouraged the faculty to make church visits a standard part of our future field trips. "We should visit a subset of local churches each trip to update them on the project and encourage their participation in the effort". As lunch ended, I asked the students to consider how the community might view teachers, police officers, planners, and other civil servants serving their neighborhood who never, during their long tenures in the community, made the effort to attend local services? Without exception, the students felt such behavior would raise serious questions regarding their cultural sensitivity severely undermining their local community service efforts.

Two weeks after our students' orientation trip, we returned to staff WIPNO's first community planning forum attended by more than fifty residents. As in Emerson Park and Lansdowne, we started the forum by engaging residents in the preparation of an initial community conditions map. Using large base maps, colored markers, and stickers residents quickly generated a large number of significant neighborhood assets, problem areas, and untapped resources. We also asked each person to do something we had not done during previous neighborhood planning processes. We asked them to write down their single most desired outcome for the planning process that we subsequently organized into common themes. In doing so, we explained our plan to use these ideas to formulate a preliminary vision statement for the Winstanley/ Industry Park Neighborhood Improvement Plan.

As the meeting ended, we invited residents to share their feedback on the forum as well as suggestions for making future meetings more educational, productive, and fun. Finally, we asked those present to assist our team in further documenting existing neighborhood conditions using disposable cameras as we had previously done in the Lansdowne neighborhood. We then provided each volunteer with a caption book to be used to briefly describe each of their photos categorizing each image as a neighborhood strength, weakness, or untapped resource.

In the days following the WIPNO planning forum, approximately forty-five residents took time to "shoot the neighborhood" using disposable cameras. While this was going on, several graduate research assistants worked with the principal of the neighborhood's largest middle school to carry out a complimentary planning activity. We involved thirty middle-school students in a two-part activity to elicit their perceptions of the neighborhood. Students were organized into teams and asked to generate as many positive qualities or characteristics of a "Great Neighborhood." As students named a positive characteristic, their teams were given a point and rewarded with small chocolate bars. By the end of the exercise, the teams had generated more than fifty positive qualities of a "Great Neighborhood" (while consuming dozens of Hershey candy bars).

We then generated a composite list of characteristics that local children used to describe the ideal neighborhood. We invited the students to take a large piece of drawing paper and a box of colored markers to create what we called the "Spike Lee: The Good, the Bad, and It's Gotta Go Now, Baby Mural." Students folded their drawing paper into three equally sized vertical panels and drew on the first panel, the absolute best "place, space, thing, or person" in the neighborhood. On the second panel they drew the absolute worst "place, space, thing, or person" in the neighborhood. On the third panel they drew an image of what they would like to see their "worst" drawing replaced by if they were Mayor of East St. Louis for a day.

We described how their images would be organized into an attractive exhibition in the entranceway of their school where

WIPNO's second community planning forum was scheduled to place in mid-October. The room became extremely quiet as our young planners put their "thinking caps" on to begin the process of sharing their perspectives on Winstanley/Industry Park. While the students worked on their murals, several graduate research assistants took their photographs and asked them a few biographical questions. This information was subsequently used to create three by four-inch identification plaques for each of their murals.

The students' artwork featured an extraordinary range of images! Among those depicting the neighborhood's "best" features were drawings of the Mississippi River, Gateway Arch, Wesley Bethel United Methodist Church, Mt. Sinai Missionary Baptist Church, Rep. Wyvetter Younge, and the East St. Louis Olympians—Florence Joyner and Jackie Joyner-Kersee. Among the "worst" drawings were images of the recently abandoned Ober-Nestor glass factory, vacant storefronts, and illegal-dump sites. Among the "future visions" drawings were a lush community garden, a renovated public library, a state-of-the-art playground, rehabilitated row houses, and a farmer market. Of the thirty murals produced by the students, the most powerful one depicted a young girl exiting the Miles Davis Elementary School surrounded by a dark cloud of reddish smoke coming from a building marked - paint factory. The student's caption read, "Tanya is sick! We all know why! Won't you help her?"

In the leadup to the October planning forum we used the most successful outreach strategies from our Emerson Park and Lansdowne experiences to drive residents to the planning meeting. As was our custom, we also organized a group of students and residents to door knock the neighborhood inviting each head of household, small business owner, and municipal/social service agency director to the event. During these activities, we highlighted the opportunity those attending the meeting would have to review "resident" rather than "outside professional" assessments of existing neighborhood conditions and future development possibilities. We also let people know that we would be discussing the more than 1,000 photos recently taken by their neighbors. Finally, we informed them that thirty "future possibilities" drawings generated by area middle schoolers would also be exhibited at the meeting.

More than sixty-five neighborhood residents attended WIPNO's October planning forum. Many of these individuals came early to inspect the children's drawings that were carefully hung in the school foyer. My workshop students were delighted to see the young artists who had produced these images directing their families to their drawings, pointing to the small plaques featuring their personal biographies, and posing for family pictures in front of their individual murals. Parents, teachers, and residents viewing these images appeared deeply moved by the students' thoughtful insights and powerful depictions of their community's many treasures, challenges, and possibilities.

Using a "four shoe box activity," the graduate research assistants asked stakeholders to work in groups to examine a subset of approximately 1,000 photographs their neighbors had taken since the last forum. Each group was asked to categorize the photos as current strengths and weaknesses or future development opportunities or threats. After each group categorized approximately 100 images, they organized the photos based upon common themes. For example, photos of attractive residential housing reflecting various architectural styles were organized under the theme "solid/historic building stock" and placed in the "community assets category." Images of abandoned rail lines, warehouses, and factories were organized under the theme, "deindustrialization/joblessness" and placed under the "community problems category." Photos of a former used car lot, closed convenience store, and abandoned food processing factory were organized under the theme of "prime development sites" and placed under the "future opportunities category." Photos of the only functioning library, a portion of which had already been closed, were organized under the theme of "at risk community facilities" and placed under the "future threats category."

After this activity, the residents reconvened as a single assembly to hear our students share the results of their historical and demographic research. Local stakeholders were delighted to be reminded of the many civic improvement and municipal reform movements that had been initiated by Winstanley/Industry Park residents. They also appreciated the students' recognition of the many socially minded local businesses that had made significant contributions to local economic and community development. Among these was the funeral home established by former Mayor Carl Officer's grandfather, who made it possible for dozens of local students to go away to college. On the other hand, they were quite troubled by the low educational attainment and workforce participation data and elevated unemployment and poverty rates cited by the students. Following the student presentation, local stakeholders took time to discuss the various data they had reviewed. This discussion focused on steps the neighborhood along with municipal, county, state, and federal agencies could take to replace the scores of manufacturing jobs they and their neighbors had seen disappear.

Before adjourning the meeting, Rev. Wilson asked those present to share their ideas regarding how to improve future meetings. One resident proposed rotating the location of future meetings to make it easier for people from different parts of the community to attend. Another resident felt this would be a good idea because it would give other local institutions, in addition to Wesley Bethel United Methodist and the Miles Davis School, a stake in the process. Rev. Herman Watson, the newly appointed pastor of Mt. Sinai Missionary Baptist, agreed to host WIPNO's November planning forum. At the end of the meeting, I distributed copies of the land use, building condition, and site maintenance survey and urban infrastructure conditions survey, explaining that our students and faculty would be using these instruments to collect parcel and street level data regarding current physical conditions within the neighborhood. Before adjourning we invited local stakeholders interested in this aspect of the process to join our students in collecting these data during the next two weeks.

The participation of Professors Andrejasich and Orland in the Winstanley/ Industry Park planning process resulted in two significant improvements in our physical conditions survey activities. With Andrejasich's help we developed easy-to-use operational definitions for each of the physical conditions survey's major variables. We then developed a 100-slide photographic show to help students develop a consistent approach to applying these more clearly defined standards. After orienting our students to the goals, objectives, and methods of physical condition surveying, including the use of our survey instruments, we asked them to use the revised survey, complete with our new working definitions, to evaluate ten individual properties from slides they were being shown. This process was repeated, ten property slides at a time, until the students produced highly consistent results. Realizing the difference between evaluating a structure in the comfort of a high-tech laboratory versus in a low-income urban neighborhood, we then took our student surveyors to a distressed neighborhood near the UIUC campus to better prepare them for the challenges of collecting accurate data in the field.

With Brian Orland's assistance we made a second improvement in our physical conditions surveying. Brian encouraged us to adapt the standard machine-readable data forms our campus regularly used for course evaluations to collect the land use, building conditions, site condition, and urban infrastructure data we needed. Following Prof. Orland's advice, we substituted the course evaluation questions typically found on these forms with our physical conditions survey questions. Using a single form to evaluate the conditions of an individual building parcel, we were able to eliminate the time-consuming process of "keystroking" our field observations recorded on paper forms into digital Excel spreadsheets. Using this new system, our students carefully recorded their building/parcel observations on modified machine-readable "scantron" forms. When they returned to campus, we submitted the entire set of 1,600 surveys to our campus's Information Technology Center that used digital reading equipment to produce an error-free Excel database that we subsequently used to produce basic descriptive statistics on existing building and infrastructure conditions. In addition, using the unique block and lot number from this spreadsheet to geo-code our land use and urban infrastructure data, we were able to generate highly reliable thematic maps of the Winstanley/Industry Park neighborhood within a few days of completing our fieldwork. This creative use of existing campus technology allowed us to produce more reliable physical conditions data in a fraction of the time.

In late October, we were able to successfully survey 1,600 building parcels and 220 street lengths in the Winstanley/Industry Park neighborhood. With this information, Prof. Orland and his landscape architecture students were able to use GIS software to produce an elegant set of thematic maps highlighting the most important features of Winstanley/Industry Park's built environment. While revealing a large number of vacant building parcels and deteriorated buildings, the maps also highlighted a wide variety of local land uses, including: industrial, transportation, utilities, commercial, municipal/ social services, and residential. The data also documented a large number of property owners who had made recent improvements to their properties notwithstanding the ongoing "redlining" affecting the neighborhood.

At WIPNO's December planning forum, seventy-five local stakeholders discussed the physical conditions data we had collected; reviewed an institutional leaders' survey instrument and a local residents' interview schedule. Participants suggested a series of improvements to these instruments. Among these were recommendations to provide interviewees with a simple map of the study area to help them better understand the exact geography we were investigating; the rewording of many questions emphasizing the use of simpler "non-planner-ese" language; the movement of questions requesting personal information, such as household incomes, to the end of the survey, and a significant shortening of the instrument.

In early February of 1992, students from my workshop, assisted by Professors Andrejasich, Orland and Selby's studios made two multi-day trips to East St. Louis to interview local officials and residents regarding their perceptions of current neighborhood conditions and future development possibilities. Many of these interviews were conducted with local leaders who volunteered to participate in this phase of the planning process. The students who conducted these joint interviews noted a number of ways in which resident participation enhanced the interviewing process. First, local residents were much more likely to grant our students interviews if they were accompanied by a resident, especially someone they appeared to know and respect. Second, local residents were more likely to provide in-depth answers to questions when prompted by neighborhood residents whose contextual knowledge enabled them to ask very specific follow-up questions related to the who, what, when, why, and how of the situations being discussed.

At WIPNO's February planning forum our students presented the interview results to nearly eighty residents. Their report highlighted stakeholders' appreciation of the neighborhood's many assets, including its central location, successful businesses, engaged congregations, strong homeownership groups, and civic-minded residents. Stakeholders took pride in the public service legacies of several of its long-standing businesses including the local Head Start based at Wesley United Methodist and the recently launched neighborhood cleanup and watch program spearheaded by local churches under the name of Operation New Spirit.

There were also serious concerns regarding the neighborhood's future. Among these were a significant drop in local homeownership; residents' and business owners' difficulties securing credit for real estate purchases and improvements; escalating street violence related to illegal drug sales; ongoing loss of neighborhood-oriented retail businesses; overextension of the city's social service delivery system; poor quality public schools; and deteriorating public infrastructure. The students finished their presentation emphasizing residents' and leaders' strong belief in the neighborhood's ability to capitalize on its central location, history of effective collective action, strong network of community-minded churches and businesses to successfully implement a revitalization strategy focused on local economic development, residential housing improvement, infrastructure repair and maintenance, enhanced community/police cooperation, and expanded services for children and families, especially in the area of substance abuse prevention, intervention, and treatment.

Professors Andrejasich, Orland, and Selby's students outlined their proposals for upgrading the St. Clair County Head Start playground at Rev. Wilson's church and carrying out ESLARP's first residential home repair project. Using Sketch-Up, a basic computer visualization software package, the landscape architecture and architecture students highlighted the dramatic improvements that could be achieved in the appearance and functionality of these two properties through a basic "scrape up/paint up" treatment. Residents smiled and applauded the "after" images of the Head Start playground that was to be enlarged by twenty-five percent, made safer through the addition of an improved ground cover and a new fence, and made more enjoyable through the repair of existing playground equipment and the construction of a new picnic pavilion. They also applauded the improvements to be made to the home of one of the neighborhood's elders. The "after" images for this building highlighted the scraping, priming and repainting of the structure's exterior, installation of a new roof, repair of the front porch and planting of new shrubs and flowers.

The students described how they had worked with the Head Start board of directors and the local residents to determine the work to be completed at each site. They went on to discuss how they had secured the bulk of the needed building and plant materials for these projects from UIUC alumni employed in the construction industry and had "pulled" the needed permits with the help of Township Supervisor McGaughey and Rep. Younge. They concluded their presentation by inviting residents with landscape installation and building construction knowledge and equipment to join them during the second weekend of April to complete these projects.

Professor Andrejasich and Don Johnson, graduate research assistant in architecture, at the site of the St. Clair County Head Start worksite (Photo by K. Reardon)

Michelle Whetten supervising neighborhood youth working on the expansion of the St. Clair County Head Start playground (Photo by ESLARP Staff)

The residents and students attending the meeting were excited to be initiating these two modest, but highly visible, projects that had been chosen by those participating in the planning process. The students were confident these improvement projects would help convince local cynics that the neighborhood planning process was more than "performance art." They were also cautiously optimistic that their neighborhood improvement actions in a city experiencing severe economic decline would attract the interest and capital of interested outsiders. More than a dozen local tradesmen, as well as several dozen-neighborhood volunteers, committed themselves to participating in the playground and home improvement efforts in late April.

More than fifty volunteers successfully expanded and upgraded the St. Clair County Head Start playground at Wesley United Methodist in late April and completed repairs and beautification efforts at the home of a senior citizen with disabilities. The local craftsman and university students who worked on these projects were thrilled by the transformative impact these modest projects had on the two targeted properties. They were especially pleased when area residents unexpectedly appeared at the work sites, picked up tool belts, and joined the construction process.

The "expanded and improved" St. Clair County Head Start Playground at the Wesley Bethel United Methodist Church (Photo by K. Reardon)

The positive buzz these projects generated prompted more than ninety local residents to participate in the neighborhood summit held in May in nearby Centreville. Following breakfast, those participating in the summit spent the morning reviewing and discussing the historical, demographic, physical conditions, and stakeholders' interview data collected by our students. After a spirited discussion of the planning implications of these data, stakeholders spent the remainder of the morning revising a preliminary draft of an overall development goal (i.e. mission statement) and a list of ten neighborhood improvement objectives that WIPNO's Executive Committee had formulated based upon their review of these data.

After considerable discussion, summit participants agreed to have the following statement serve as their plan's overall development goal:

> The residents and leaders of the historic Winstanley/Industry Park community, led by the Winstanley/Industry Park Neighborhood Organization, seek to: arrest the area's social, economic, and physical decline; meet the basic quality of life needs of current and future residents and businesses; and lay the foundation

for active community involvement by comprehensively planning for the neighborhood's human and physical development.

Having come to a consensus in support of this overall development goal, the participating residents and leaders identified the following seven neighborhood improvement objectives to help them achieve their overall development goal.

1. To enhance public health and safety by implementing infrastructure repair and housing demolition programs.

2. To stabilize the existing residential building stock by reducing operating costs by assisting owners in making needed repairs.

3. To improve the neighborhood's physical appearance and functioning through the implementation of an integrated urban design scheme.

4. To expand local business activity by aggressively pursuing small business assistance and job training programs.

5. To reduce alcohol and drug abuse by developing a comprehensive community-based substance abuse prevention, intervention, and treatment program.

6. To aggressively pursue campaigns to make City, County, and State policies more responsive to the needs of the city's older residential neighborhoods such as Winstanley/ Industry Park.

7. To establish a permanent organization to empower local residents to address their neighborhood's social and economic problems.

While the policy objectives related to public health, housing rehabilitation, urban design, economic development, and substance abuse paralleled those identified in both the Emerson Park and Lansdowne neighborhood improvement plans, the importance given to grassroots organizing (Objective 7) and public interest (i.e. policy reform) campaigns (Objective 6) distinguished this plan from these earlier documents. Having watched public officials ignore high quality plans that hundreds of local residents had worked together in the Emerson Park and Lansdowne neighborhoods, to create, local residents were acutely aware of the need to approach their planning in a manner that would build a broad base of non-partisan political support for their proposals. They sought to achieve this outcome by viewing all of their interviewing and outreach activities as opportunities to both collect good data and to motivate local residents, business owners, and institutional leaders to join WIPNO. In doing so, they hoped to transform WIPNO from a small voluntary association representing a handful of area churches into a broad-based citizen organization with sufficient non-partisan political clout to insure the adoption of their planning and development proposals by city, state, and federal officials.

Summit participants reviewed the plan's seven neighborhood improvement objectives identifying the one that most interested them. After doing so, they were invited to join other residents interested in that same objective at nearby tables. Two area professionals with extensive planning, programming, and development experience in their policy area were present at each table. Graduate

Local stakeholders, students, and faculty working together at the WIPNO neighborhood summit (Photo by ESLARP Staff).

research assistants who were serving as facilitators of these break-out sessions then invited their group to participate in a "blue sky exercise" during which time they were challenged to generate as many policies, programs, or projects ideas that could, under the right circumstances, help the neighborhood achieve this objective. They strongly encouraged the group to think "outside of the box," caution-ing them against killing a good idea before its potential could be ful-ly considered. Once the breakout session participants had exhausted their inventories of ideas, the two professionals in their groups were given the opportunity to provide quick feedback on the viability/feasibility of each proposal given the current funding environment within the region. These professionals did so by giving each sugges-tion a "thumbs up," a "maybe/maybe not," or a "thumbs down" hand signal along with a one-minute explanation of their assessments.

Within minutes of receiving these instructions, the room filled with conversation, laughter, and gentle ribbing as participants shared dozens of conventional, as well as novel, improvement proposals. Those participating in the breakout sessions generated more than 100 economic and community development ideas that were neatly recorded on large sheets of newsprint hanging near each table. Once they had shared and recorded each of their proposals, the two invit-ed (substantive) policy experts were invited to share their "real time" feedback on these ideas. An unexpected outcome of this process was the number of significant planning, technical assistance and funding commitments these agency representatives made, in the event, WIP-NO chose to pursue initiatives of interest to them and their agencies. After thanking the policy experts for their assessments, the graduate research assistants invited each of the breakout session participants to use the five green stickers and the one red "skull and cross-bones" sticker to highlight the five policies, plans, and projects they believed could best advance the neighborhood's community development ef-forts within their programmatic area. Finally, the facilitators invited those sitting at their table to use their single "skull and cross-bones" sticker to identify the proposal they most adamantly opposed. With these instructions, members of each group used their dots and skull and cross-bones to indicate their planning preferences in their adopted policy area.

We had not previously used this method to elicit local residents' programming ideas and development preferences but it now generated dozens of interesting environmental, economic, and community development proposals. WIPNO was then able to reduce this list to fifty-three neighborhood improvement proposals enjoying a broad base of community support. These items were subsequently organized into immediate, intermediate, and long-term project lists that subsequently formed the basis of *The Winstanley/Industry Park Neighborhood Improvement Plan* that WIPNO distributed, following approval by its executive committee, to local stakeholders in July of 1992. Among the programmatic highlights of this 400-plus page document were:

1. An emergency manhole cover initiative to replace thirty-eight covers adjacent to important community facilities such as schools, libraries, and senior centers;

2. Re-establishment of an effective animal control program to address the increasing problem of abandoned dogs and cats;

3. A new storm water control strategy to mitigate the neighborhood's recurring flooding problems featuring traditional (pipes and drains) and non-traditional (grading. swales, and grey water recycling) elements;

4. A senior citizen home rehabilitation initiative to stabilize and improve single-family residences occupied by low-income seniors that are at-risk for abandonment;

5. A farmers' market proposal to provide Winstanley/Industry Park and other downtown East St. Louis neighborhoods access to healthy, affordable, and culturally-appropriate foods;

6. Project Read/Algebra Project to enhance the basic literacy and numeracy skills of East St. Louis residents seeking to secure living wage employment;

7. A "buy local" initiative to encourage municipal agencies and non-profit institutions to increase the percentage of their regular purchases made from businesses and venders operating within the city and region;

8. Establishment of a teen and young adult substance abuse prevention, intervention, and treatment program modeled on the Therapeutic Community of America's model reflected in the work of The Outreach Project in Jamaica, New York.

WIPNO's executive committee subsequently approved the plan and asked UIUC faculty to continue working with their neighborhood during the 1992-1993 academic year to accomplish three things: the formal incorporation of WIPNO as a general purpose economic and community development organization serving Winstanley/Industry Park neighborhood; formulation of a five-year implementation strategy to complete the immediate-term projects contained in the plan; and finally, the pursuit of additional (higher-impact) neighborhood improvement projects to maintain and further expand stakeholder participation in this exciting new resident-led community transformation initiative.

Sensing strong community and campus interest in continuing to work together to transform the proposals contained in the plan into concrete projects offering tangible benefits local residents, ESLARP's faculty advisory committee decided to continue its planning activities in the Winstanley/Industrial Park neighborhood during the next academic year.

Following the faculty advisory committee's decision to continue its partnership with WIPNO for another academic year, four graduate planning students, who had just completed the first year of UIUC's Master in Regional Planning Program, Rafael Cestero, Karna Gerich, Kirk Goodrich, and Juan Salgado, offered to make the development of the five-year implementation strategy for WIPNO's Neighborhood Improvement Plan the focus of their master's capstone Project.

During the 1992-1993 academic year these highly motivated students worked together to expand resident involvement in WIPNO; identify and train WIPNO's Executive Committee in the fundamentals of community-based planning and development; recruit volunteers from UIUC's Law Clinic to complete WIPNO's state charitable organization registration and IRS 501c3 Application establishing it as a tax-exempt and tax-deductible non-profit; and complete the

191-page *Winstanley/Industry Park Neighborhood Organization's Five-Year Neighborhood Demonstration Area Strategic Community Stabilization Plan.*

The implementation strategy these students formulated was noteworthy in a number of ways. First, it was pursued in a highly participatory approach that significantly increased the number of residents, especially youth, participating in WIPNO's activities. Secondly, it presented detailed descriptions, rationales, action steps, cost estimates, funding sources, and technical assistance requirements for five "signature" community development projects designed to enable WIPNO to successfully implement. Thirdly, it offered a comprehensive analysis of concentrated poverty featuring place, people, and labor market factors as the basis for their team's poverty reduction program that featured: physical rehabilitation and development; human and capital resource development; citizen participation; leadership development; and human capital development proposals. Finally, the plan presented a phasing strategy in which the geographic core of the neighborhood would be stabilized during the first five years of the plan in order to create the momentum needed to address the challenges facing the community's more highly distressed peripheral areas during two subsequent five-year periods.

The work need to produce ESLARP's neighborhood stabilization implementation plan proceeded with great intensity during the 1992-1993 academic year as more than one hundred and fifty undergraduate and graduate architecture, landscape architecture, and urban and regional planning students worked with WIPNO's executive committee and area residents to successfully complete two of ESLARP's most celebrated projects – the construction of the Illinois Avenue Playground and the establishment of the East St. Louis Farmers' Market.

8. THE ILLINOIS AVENUE PLAYGROUND AND EARNING OUR LICENSE TO OPERATE

AS OUR SECOND-YEAR GRADUATE planning students began convening local stakeholders to develop the outline for WIPNO's neighborhood stabilization implementation strategy, Elder Earl Dobbins Jr. of Wesley Bethel United Methodist asked them to meet with seniors from the nearby 19th precinct. Following a short ride that took them outside of the Winstanley/Industry Park study area, they arrived at an immaculate cottage on Illinois Avenue owned by Dr. William and Dorothy Kinney, long-time pillars of the city's faith-based, civil rights, and medical communities. Following a short round of introductions, Dr. Kinney and his wife invited Dobbins and our team to walk with them to the nearby intersection of Illinois avenue and 19th street.

Dr. Kinney pointed to a large vacant lot that he described as a long-time community eyesore and trouble spot. He explained how an outside investor with no visible ties to the city had purchased the three lots, along with the shotgun styled bungalow that sat on the edge of this 30,000 square foot property. Marie Drake, a community leader who, along with several other residents had joined the group, described how the owner had neglected the property by failing to mow the grass, trim the bushes, and secure the deteriorating bungalow. Drake went on to explain how local addicts used the building to take drugs and how a teenage girl from the neighborhood had recently been sexually assaulted in the building. The recurring use of the building and its grounds for illegal drug use, according to Dr. Kinney, had destroyed residents' peace of mind preventing many of them from allowing their children to play outside. "Every time I look out my kitchen window at that abandoned building and unkempt property, I am reminded of the price our children pay for its presence in our neighborhood", stated Minnie Reed a neighbor who had joined the conversation.

One of the students noted, "The owner has posted a 'do not trespass' sign on the property to discourage those who might want to use it for illegal activities. Certainly, that shows a certain level of community concern on his part." Dr. Kinney smiled at our student, explaining how he had recently led a group of octogenarians in cleaning up the lot after repeated efforts to contact the owner had failed. He said the "do not trespass" sign appeared within days of the residents' cleanup demonstrating the owner's contempt for him and his neighbors. As the group walked back to Dr. Kinney's home, he requested their assistance in helping area residents secure site control of the lot and demolish the bungalow so the parcels could be transformed into a safe and attractive play space for children. "What could be more powerful in demonstrating our neighborhood's vitality than a successful effort to turn one of its most hideous eyesores and notorious crime spots into a beautiful place for children and adults to interact?" Moved by his appeal, the students explained that they worked under the direction of WIPNO's executive committee whose members decide which community development projects would be undertaken by the organization. While acknowledging the importance of projects such as this, they pointed out that it was located outside of WIPNO's study area and they were barely keeping up with their current community planning responsibilities. Dr. Kinney responded by saying, "You look like a very capable group. Plus, I bet you have friends on campus who would be willing to lend a hand for a worthwhile project such as this."

Upon their return to campus, the students discussed their meeting with Dr. Kinney and his neighbors with ESLARP's faculty advisory committee whose members were excited about the project. They felt it would offer students a terrific opportunity to work on a meaningful design/build project as part of an interdisciplinary team, however, they believed WIPNO's executive committee would be unlikely agree to pursue the project given its location outside of their neighborhood.

What we failed to understand was Dr. Kinney's extraordinary standing within the community. During the Jim Crow era,

Dr. Kinney was responsible for delivering and caring for more African-American babies than any other doctor within the region. His clinical knowledge and skills, along with his commitment to promoting health and wellness within the city were legendary.

WIPNO's executive committee voted unanimously to extend their service area six blocks so the playground site could be considered part of the Winstanley/ Industry Park neighborhood. During the discussion of the project, the students learned that Dr. Kinney had delivered the majority of WIPNO's executive committee as well as several members of the city council.

Shortly after WIPNO decided to undertake the Illinois Avenue playground project, the faculty advisory committee convened a meeting of the urban planning, architecture, and landscape architecture studios working in the city. The overwhelming majority of those participating in these classes voiced their enthusiastic support for the project and strong desire to contribute to the effort. The following week, students representing each of our East St. Louis studios met with Dr. Kinney and his neighbors to discuss their goals for the project. They toured, measured, and documented the site's major physical features; met with St. Clair County Tax Assessor's office to determine who owned the properties; and conferred with the City of East St. Louis City Manager's office to understand how the proposed park site was currently zoned, and the process residents would have to follow to acquire and develop the site as a playground.

Dr. Kinney and his wife's passion for their neighborhood and its children quickly captured our students' hearts. By the end of our meeting, the students working on the project appeared willing to travel to hell and back to make the Illinois Avenue playground a reality! Their subsequent visit to the site further reinforced their interest in the project—they were taken by the once grand "City Beautiful" boulevard the playground faced as well as the elegant collection of Arts and Crafts homes surrounding the site. Finally, they loved the collection of ancient live oak trees clustered at the center of the site, its excellent natural drainage, as well as the design challenges presented by the presence of a significantly damaged bungalow.

Their visit to the St. Clair County Assessor's office produced dramatic news—it appeared as though the proposed playground property was on the county's auction list because of the owner's failure to pay his taxes. The property's tax-delinquent status would enable WIPNO to either bid on the property at an open auction or to arrange a sole source contract to purchase the property for a modest fee of five dollars a linear foot (i.e. $500). Upon acquisition, WIPNO would either have to pay the back taxes owed to local taxing districts with interests in the parcel or secure the forgiveness of these past due taxes from these bodies before pursuing the site's redevelopment.

The team's visit to the East St. Louis City Manager's office was also encouraging. The city manager informed our team that their proposal to transform these vacant parcels into a neighborhood playground was an "as of right" use under the city's zoning ordinance. This was great news! This meant that Dr. Kinney and his neighbors would not have to secure a "use variance" to repurpose these vacant lots as a playground. The city manager encouraged WIPNO and our student team to return after they had secured title to the property from St. Clair County and prepared a preliminary site plan meeting local and state regulations. When these tasks were accomplished, the city manager pledged to do all he could to facilitate the approval of the site plan, a positive environmental review, and a finding of no conflict with state historic preservation regulations so the playground project could move forward.

Our student team convened a second meeting of the studios working on the project to prepare a preliminary work plan for completing the playground. With the assistance of Professors Andrejasich and Orland the studios formulated a common vision, development objectives, design guidelines, work plan, cost estimates, and tentative schedule to complete the project by May 1993. The students hoped to finalize the acquisition, site planning, conceptual design, architectural drawings, and regulatory approval of the project by the end of the fall semester of 1992. They believed they could accomplish these objectives by organizing the studios to pursue three independently but carefully coordinated work plans.

As the fall semester of 1992 ended, representatives of the studios working on the playground travelled to East St. Louis to present a preliminary draft of their master plan for the Illinois Avenue Playground to leaders from the 19th Precinct Citizens Committee and WIPNO. Those participating in this meeting were delighted with the students' plan that featured an attractive entranceway sign as well as a system of curvilinear paths dividing the 29,000 square foot playground into unique activity spaces (i.e. outdoor rooms). Among the proposed improvements was a stage built into the side of the bungalow that would remain as a storage facility; a double-dutch platform; a shaded picnic area with checker board/chess boards embedded in the tops of several tables; a children's play space featuring swings, seesaws, a climbing structure, a sliding pond; and a semi-protected space for seniors.

But Elder Dobbins got up to challenge the process. "I like the design but let's face it—I am no spring chicken! How do we know what the children in our neighborhood want? We know that if the playground doesn't meet their needs; they are simply not going to use it. If they don't, we know who will—local drug dealers! Before we go ahead and build something, we might like, but our children and grandchildren may not—why don't we slow down a bit in order to bring them into the process?" Slightly embarrassed by our failure to follow our own participatory planning principles, the faculty agreed to work with local leaders to facilitate several forums offering neighborhood youth the opportunity to shape the final design of this new public recreation space.

In mid-January the principal of the Miles Davis elementary school arranged for a small group of architecture and landscape architecture students, under the direction of Jeanne Genis to meet with two groups of twenty-five middle schoolers who lived near the proposed playground site. These UIUC students showed the middle schoolers slides of several of the region's most popular playgrounds. Jeanne then asked the children what they liked most and least about each of these facilities. She then invited the students to draw the elements/activity areas/structures they would most like to see incorporated into the proposed Illinois Avenue playground.

The students produced a fantastic array of playground ideas, including: a monster-themed miniature golf course, a climbable version of Eero Saarinen's nearby Gateway Arch, a massive water slide, community garden plots, and a petting zoo featuring a cooperatively-owned and maintained pony. As the students completed their drawings, they were asked if we could display them in the school's main corridor during the coming week. The UIUC students explained how each Miles Davis student would be given a "smiley face decal" to vote for the feature they most wanted to see incorporated within the proposed playground.

The UIUC students then invited those most interested in continuing their involvement in the design process to join them in two weeks at Mt. Sinai Missionary Baptist Church to prepare a preliminary site plan. Two weeks later eighteen middle schoolers joined a small group of UIUC students and faculty at Rev. Watson's church to produce a preliminary site plan for the Illinois Avenue Playground. When the middle schoolers entered the church's all-purpose room, they immediately noticed a large piece of green felt covering most of the floor as well as a set of large red felt "cut-outs" reflecting the most popular playground ideas generated during our initial Miles Davis school planning workshop. The UIUC students informed the middle schoolers that it was their job to arrange all of the proposed improvements on the green felt that was sized to reflect the playground site's actual dimensions.

The UIUC landscape architecture students distributed a checklist of "things to remember" when trying to create a special place based upon urban design principles popularized MIT's Kevin Lynch. The handout encouraged the students to consider the:

- Creation of an attractive **entranceway** that welcomes visitors to the space, announces its purpose, and identifies the owners/stewards of the property;

- Establishment of clear **borders** separating this important recreation and cultural space from its surrounding properties;

- Designation of **specific areas** within the playground dedicated to such activities, as: playing checkers, practicing double-dutch, growing fruits and vegetables, presenting musical and theatrical events;

- Development of an **internal circulation system** that allows visitors, regardless of age or infirmity, to easily travel from one section of the playground to another;

- Display of a **short history** of this neighborhood as well as the origins and evolution of the playground project; and,

- Maintenance of **clear views** of the playground's interior spaces to allow residents, passersby, and the police to monitor the area for public safety purposes.

Following this short introduction to urban design, the children flipped through nearly two dozen improvement cut outs to gain a clearer understanding of the structures and spaces their site plan had to accommodate. Within minutes they agreed to make the corner of Illinois Avenue and 19th Street the formal entrance of the playground. They subsequently decided to establish the playground's primary walkway starting at the entranceway running diagonally through the length of the playground. Along this major walkway, they sited the playground's major play space featuring an oversized sandbox and a fort-like structure made out of a re-purposed concrete sewer pipe section. Along the main walkway towards the rear of the playground, the children proposed a beautiful seating area for elders complete with park benches, raised flowerbeds and a small fountain.

The students carried cut outs to the appropriate spots on the green felt in order to evaluate how they might relate to adjacent uses. Everything appeared to be going along well until a young girl proposed the placement of the playground's sliding pond immediately behind the elderly seating area. Nervous about the possibility of a rapidly descending student "missile" taking out one of the neighborhood's elders, I gently suggested increasing the distance between these two "incompatible" playground uses. However, each time I turned around this young girl had moved these two proposed improvements back together. After my second attempt to establish a reasonable buffer between the children's slide and the elderly sitting area, the young girl blew up at me saying, "You don't understand ANYTHING, if my grandmother doesn't have a place to sit in the middle of this playground then she and my parents will never let me play here, because they will think its unsafe." With full conviction and in a very loud voice she then proceeded to criticize our proposal to build a vault-like storage shed featuring iron bars on the doors and windows. Pointing to the cutout representing this improvement she said, "This looks like Fort Knox. People will think there is gold in the shed, instead of a bunch of ten dollar basketballs and volleyballs, inviting every neighborhood addict to break into this structure."

Initially stung by the girl's unbridled critique of our design, we quickly realized that she knew more about her community than we did and was in possession of what Clifford Geertz described as important local knowledge that could significantly improve our design for this important community facility. In response to her criticisms, our students and faculty stopped micromanaging the middle schoolers.

Using the life-size site plan the middle schoolers had generated as their basic guide, UIUC architecture and landscape architecture students prepared an attractive display board presenting the site plan and a set of power points slides illustrating the participatory process the youth had used to produce this work. A few weeks later, several of the middle school students who had participated in the design process presented these materials at a WIPNO meeting held at Rev. Watson's church. Those attending the meeting were thrilled to see neighborhood youth presenting an attractive playground design. The students' presentation was followed by a series of questions from residents that were very positively structured—acknowledging some aspect of the children's design while raising thoughtful questions aimed at challenging them to further refine their preliminary ideas.

Following their presentation, Dobbins congratulated them on their work offering a motion to approve their playground design by acclamation. Everyone attending the meeting raised their hands in support of their proposal and offered the children an enthusiastic round of applause. Rev. Watson informed me that I was definitely on my way to hell. Chuckling, I said that I couldn't disagree with his prediction, but wanted to understand the theological basis for his assessment. He explained, "By organizing the children of the village to pressure their elders to build a park. You realize that we are going to have to find a way to build this playground." I responded by saying, "If one has to suffer the fires of hell, this is clearly a cause worth the pain and suffering."

In the weeks following their initial presentation, the middle school students gave encore performances of their playground presentation before two neighborhood churches whose members pledged to assist them in making the Illinois Avenue playground a reality. Members of these congregations volunteered to secure a "bush hog" mower to clear the site where grasses, bushes, and shrubs had gotten out of control. They also agreed to collect other equipment, tools, and trucks needed for the build out. In addition, they committed themselves to recruiting craftsman from the community willing to donate part or all of the weekend to support the area youth and UIUC students who would be doing most of the construction work. Finally, they offered to contact local food stores, restaurants, caterers, and congregations for donations needed to feed the more than 100 community and campus volunteers expected to participate in the event.

As WIPNO and its allies engaged in these activities, UIUC landscape architecture students worked together to finalize the playground's overall design based upon the local middle schoolers' vision. At the same time, UIUC architecture students focused their attention on preparing the many construction drawings and recruiting the volunteer craftsman needed to fabricate each of the playground's improvements (i.e. park benches, sliding pond, double-dutch platform, puppetry stage, etc.). These two teams also prepared detailed work plans, staffing recommendations, materials/ supplies inventories, and tools and equipment lists needed to complete the playground's many physical elements. They also reached out to their respective alumni networks to request donations of plant materials, hardware, and lumber. In the end, nearly a dozen construction-related businesses operated by UIUC alumni donated dozens of trees, hundreds of shrubs/bushes, thousands of seasonal flowers, skids of sod and boxes of nails, bolts, and screws, and other hardware products required for the project. When a non-alum whose family has done hundreds of thousands of dollars' worth of sidewalk, street, and parking lot construction in East St. Louis heard about the project, he called to ask why he had not been asked to help. He offered to come to the site several days before the built out to install a fully ADA compliant sidewalk around the perimeter of the playground facing both Illinois Avenue and 19th Street—an expensive improvement we did not have the funds to complete.

During January, February, and March of 1993, the planning students were busy tracking down representatives of the eight separate taxing districts entitled to receive property tax revenues from the building lots upon which the playground would be built to request forgiveness of $8,000 in back taxes and forbearance of future revenues from these properties while they were being used for a public purpose. Identifying the local taxing districts was relatively easy, determining when and where they met, who chaired these meetings, and the protocols for getting on the agendas of these bodies proved to be enormously challenging.

For example, when I called the chair of the East St. Louis library board to inquire about their meeting times, places and procedures, he responded by asking, "Who wants to know?" When he subsequently refused to answer a few straightforward questions regarding their upcoming meeting, I was forced to call Rep. Younge's office for assistance. Several WIPNO leaders accompanied me to the local firehouse where the library board was meeting. When we entered their conference room, the members looked like children who had been caught smoking their first cigarettes by their parents. After introducing myself and the members of our delegation, I asked if they had a copy of their evening's agenda and could tell us when "new business" might be addressed. The chair responded by saying there was no printed meeting agenda and certainly no time for new business or public comment. Armed with a copy of the Illinois' Open Meetings Act, I informed him that he was obliged to offer us the opportunity to speak and request action on relevant matters. The chair then said we could raise our concerns following their already "packed" agenda. As it turned out, the only item on their agenda was a motion to approve travel reimbursements for several library board members who had recently attended the annual meeting of the American Library Association.

We made our presentation, and the Library Board Members appeared impressed by and supportive of the playground project. But when Elder Dobbins asked the board to forgive the slightly less than $1,500 in back taxes and a bit more than $150 a year in future tax revenues the Chair suggested the issue be tabled until he consulted the city attorney on the matter. He said, "I am not sure we have the authority to forgive back taxes and forego future revenues. While a single project, such as yours has very little impact on our budget, what would happen if other groups seeking to address blighted properties came forward seeking similar relief? This could affect our ability keep the local libraries going which is our first priority." Immediately following the meeting, the WIPNO leaders called Rep. Younge and Supervisor McGaughey who promised to work together to secure the past tax forgiveness and future tax forbearance from the Library Board.

Optimistic that we would be able to secure site control of the vacant parcels comprising the proposed playground site with the approval of the local taxing bodies, we revisited the city manager to confirm what else we would have to do in order to secure a building permit for the playground. The city manager said that as soon as soon as we secured site control of the proposed playground site from St. Clair County, he would initiate a preliminary environmental and historical review by the city.

Thanks to pressure from McGaughey and Younge, the local taxing districts took positive action on our tax forgiveness and forbearance requests. Armed with this information and our revised playground design and maintenance plan, we returned to the St. Clair County land disposition committee to request transfer of the playground parcels to WIPNO. The Committee appeared excited about the project but told us they required a $1,000,000 liability insurance policy. Without a certificate of insurance, they would be unable to convey the property to us. Rev. Wilson of Wesley Bethel United Methodist indicated that his church would be happy to add this coverage to the congregation's existing insurance program and with this commitment the Committee voted unanimously to convey the playground properties to WIPNO.

Excitement was short-lived. The city subsequently informed us that they could not complete the environment and historical reviews on the properties before the scheduled "build out" nor assist us in the demolition of the shotgun building, which their inspectors had recently determined to be a public nuisance. The graduate students who had been working on the playground on a non-stop basis were enraged. Their final playground design assumed the removal of the bungalow building that city officials had assured them they would carry out. With two weeks remaining before the scheduled build out, the city's refusal to demolish the bungalow was placing the entire project in jeopardy. After spending a frantic week seeking to identify a city certified demolition contractor who would take the structure down and land fill the debris at a reasonable price, several of our more anarchistic graduate students informed me of their plans to execute a do-it-yourself demolition using chain saws to cut the building into sections, a pick-up truck pull it to the ground, and, with a bit of accelerant to burn the remains.

My initial response to their plan was to encourage them to wear their safety goggles, stand upwind of the blaze, and put the East St. Louis fire department on speed dial. Early the next morning, I received a call from Prof. Orland who inquired, "Tell me you did not provide safety tips to UIUC students preparing to illegally demolish a building that is most likely filled with carcinogenic materials at a time when we struggling to support residents' efforts to promote good government in East St. Louis." Reminding me of how dangerous building demolitions could be, Brian encouraged me to redouble our efforts to find a registered demolition contractor to take down the bungalow. In the event we were unable to do so, he said he had prepared a variation of the children's playground design that featured sealing the building in order to use its exterior walls and side porch as an exciting teaching, performance, and art-making space—an inspired example of a skilled designer turning "lemons into lemonade."

As the build out date approached, I received a call from a local contractor, who had heard about our demolition problem. This man started the conversation by asking, "Tell me you are not working with Dr. Kinney and Elder Dobbins, both of whom are as old as dirt, to build a playground in the 19th Precinct." I told him that was exactly what we were trying to do but explained that we had a small bungalow, deemed to be a nuisance by the city, that needed to be demolished. Chuckling, Doug Borders explained how Dr. Kinney had delivered several of his children and how he and a friend, who was a licensed demolition contractor registered with the city, would be willing to pull the necessary permit, demolish the structure, and take care of the debris. When I asked him how much this would cost, he said $300-500 in gasoline. I then asked him about the "tipping fees" needed to remove the building debris from the site. He said, "We are going to take care of these materials with minimal tipping fees—trust me, we know how to do this." He informed me that he and his colleagues had already secured a valid demolition permit from the city.

Armed with documents showing the county's transfer of the playground properties to WIPNO, proof of our liability coverage, copies of our demolition contractor's license and permit, and a signed copy of our approved site plan, I returned to the city manager's office to secure a building permit for the Illinois Avenue Playground. I then returned to campus to submit appointment papers hiring our friendly contractor and his partner as visiting instructors to give a field seminar in "Building Demolition and Site Preparation" for our studio classes. Since we didn't have "demolition expenses" in the ESLARP budget, covering these costs as a teaching/learning activity was the only way we could get our contractor and his partner the gas money needed to "dig us out of the hole" regarding our bungalow problem. When I subsequently gave our contractor the paperwork to sign, he laughed saying, that he would be putting his "appointment papers as a UIUC 'professor' on his office wall." He and his demolition partner kept their promise by framing their contract which they proudly displayed in the Shell station office where they parked their equipment. Several days before the build out, my students and I visited the playground site and were delighted to see that the bungalow had been demolished, the debris placed in a nearby dumpster, and the site carefully leveled.

We were poised to mobilize the army of community and campus volunteers who had agreed to participate in the build out. As we did so, the graduate assistants in architecture made plans to assemble and store the topsoil, plant materials, lumber supplies and hardware items we had solicited at a nearby telephone company warehouse. While this process was underway, a group of landscape architecture students visited Champaign-Urbana nurseries owned by UIUC alumni to pick up thousands of dollars' worth of donated plant materials. Afterwards a small group of architecture and landscape architecture students visited the site to make sure it was free of any potentially dangerous debris and to stake out the exact locations where each improvement was to be installed.

Shortly after 5 AM on the first morning of our three-day construction weekend, a small group of planning students and I drove a van equipped with a large trailer filled with hand tools and a U-Haul truck loaded down with construction supplies to the playground site. As we approached the site at 6 AM, two women and several middle school students whom I recognized from the Miles Davis design charette greeted us. One of the mothers explained, "My son wasn't able to sleep. He said you were going to be building the playground that he and his friends designed. He said he had to be there to help. I hope it's OK. There really wasn't any way to keep him away this morning." Assuring the women that their children's presence would not be a problem, Kirk Goodrich, one of our graduate research assistants, informed the kids they would have to wear construction helmets, official Illinois Avenue Playground construction t-shirts, and work gloves (all of which were way bigger than these children). In addition, he said they would have to stay away from all of the motorized construction equipment while paying strict attention to his directions.

L.D. Ward, a local contractor, supervising youth volunteers during the "Build Out Weekend" for the Illinois Avenue Playground (Photo by ESLARP Staff).

Dr. Kinney and his wife soon appeared to inform us that volunteers from two area churches would be there shortly to serve breakfast, lunch, and dinner to our construction crew—significantly enhancing our team's efficiency by saving us several daytime trips to nearby eateries. Within the next hour, approximately forty UIUC students arrived and were put to work under the able direction of Prof. Andrejasich, who informed them of the major building efforts to be completed during the weekend build:

- Installation of bollards made from used railroad ties at the periphery of the site to prevent individuals from driving vehicles onto the playground;

- Construction of an attractive picket fence along the western and northern borders of the site to further enhance the site's security and appearance;

- Creation of a cruciform internal pathway system using landscape barrier cloth, well anchored railroad ties, and pea gravel;

- Building forms for the concrete required for the "double dutch" platform and the "checkers/chess play area";

- Construction of wooden benches comprising the core of the senior citizen garden area;

- Building a large sandbox at the center of the playground housing a section of concrete sewer pipe suitable for use as both a fort and/or climbing structure;

- Crafting an attractive entranceway featuring a large Illinois Avenue Playground sign and seasonal flowerbeds: and,

- Planting numerous flowerbeds throughout the site to differentiate activity areas and improve its overall appearance.

Before teams could undertake these tasks, graduate students cleared the tall grass and brush that had taken over the site using loppers, machetes, and lawn mowers. When this work was finished, the entire workforce gathered arm to arm at the southern edge of the construction site walking slowly northward picking up any natural or man-made debris that could cause someone to twist their ankle or could foul our construction equipment.

As dusk approached, the sixty volunteers working on the site had succeeded in clearing and leveling all of the areas where major improvements were to be made. Using gasoline-powered augers, they had also excavated the holes for the bollards, fencing, picnic tables, and garden seats. The day's biggest highlight was the appearance of dozens of neighborhood children and adults who quietly appeared, put on construction gear, and went to work. At day's end, as our students and faculty collected their equipment, tools, and supplies, Dr. Kinney and his wife visited the site. Marveling over the dramatic transformation Dorothy Kinney said, "It was so depressing looking out the kitchen window seeing a jungle. With what you have already done, I can now imagine a beautiful space that is going to give residents, especially our children; both joy and, most importantly, hope. You have no idea what this means to us!"

By noon on the second day, the students had installed most of the bollards to prevent automobiles and trucks from driving through the playground. They had also completed the playground's perimeter fencing and internal pathway system, which looked great. While the walls of the large sandbox play structure had been completed, little of the essential ingredient, namely sand, had been added. While, the senior citizen benches were only twenty-five percent completed, the team was confident the rest could be quickly fabricated now that they had mastered the basic construction technique.

By the end of the second day of construction, all of these projects had been completed as well as the footings for the poles needed to hold the playground's oversized entrance sign. As the students and faculty moved their equipment, tools, and supplies from the site, two large trucks arrived from the telephone company—one carrying topsoil, the other mulch. These materials, along with a small truckload of sod, would be put to good use on the final day of the build out as volunteers shifted their focus from constructing the "hard" elements of the site (i.e. sidewalks, bollard barriers, fencings, etc.) to implementing the playground's basic landscape design.

Before returning to the motel, community and campus volunteers assessed the progress that had been made. Feeling pressure to complete the project before our scheduled 4 pm dedication the next day—the students asked if they could skip our traditional Sunday services to ensure that we completed everything on time for the dedication. Following a brief discussion among the faculty, we decided to have a skeleton-like crew of landscape architecture students at the site to supervise the delivery and placement of the hundreds of trees, shrubs, bushes, and ornamental flowers being transported from the phone company's storage facility while the bulk of the students and faculty attended services at Rev. Watson's Mt. Sinai Missionary Baptist and Rev. Wilson's United Methodist. Before deciding to do so, we called each pastor to make sure it would be OK for us to attend services in our work clothes saving us the time needed to go back to the motel to change before returning to the playground site. Both pastors assured us that our appearance in work clothes would present no problem for the members of their congregations.

The following day, our students and faculty enjoyed a welcome break from our construction duties participating in the Sunday services of these two inspired congregations. The students and faculty were embarrassed when each pastor asked them to stand in order described the work they were doing to construct the Illinois Avenue Playground. At both churches, the students received standing ovations from the congregants. By the time the students headed over to the construction site, they were eager to put the finishing touches on the playground. Their commitment to finishing the project was significantly reinforced throughout the afternoon by members of Rev. Watson's and Wilson's congregations who had heard the students discuss their work at church that morning and decided to visit the site to offer words of encouragement and plates of food.

As the afternoon progressed increasing numbers of middle schoolers who had worked on the playground's design, began to appear. Eager to help they picked up shovels and trays of ornamental flowers, placing them where they felt they were most needed. This drove our architecture and landscape architecture students crazy! Faculty who noticed several of them getting increasingly irritated reminded them that the Illinois Avenue Playground was a resident-led planning and design project. Encouraging community ownership at each step of the planning and design process would enhance residents' feelings of ongoing stewardship over this important public space.

By mid-afternoon the volunteers were putting the final touches on the playground—laying sod over those parts of the site where the ground cover had been disturbed and erecting the large entranceway sign. The students covered the sign with a white cloth and a large green ribbon. As 4 PM approached a small group of community

Rev. Herman Watson, Pastor of Mt. Sinai Missionary Baptist, helping to construct the sandbox at the Illinois Avenue Playground. (Photo by ESLARP Staff).

residents and leaders, members of Mt. Sinai Missionary Baptist and Wesley United Methodist churches, WIPNO's executive board and UIUC students and faculty who had contributed to the project gathered at the entranceway of the newly constructed playground. Rev. Wilson began the dedication program with a short prayer in which he said, "We need each and every one of you whose hands contributed to the construction of this playground to pledge to each other and to God that you will continue to work together to insure that this place remains a safe and uplifting space for our children to play."

Following a loud "Amen," Rev. Wilson asked Dr. Kinney and his wife, Elder Dobbins, and Marie Drake to step forward to unveil the newly installed playground sign that featured the names of more than two dozen community groups, area businesses, UIUC classes, and alumni that had contributed to the playground's construction. WIPNO president Carol Perry officially opened the park by cutting the ribbon that obstructed its main walkway. As soon as the ribbon fell to the ground, dozens of neighborhood children raced down the playground's main walkway to be among the first to play in the recently constructed sandbox. The next agenda item was the throwing out of the ceremonial "first pitch" that was accomplished with the assistance of several student volunteers who tossed new footballs to an army of neighborhood youth eager to demonstrate their passing and catching prowess. Rep. Younge concluded the dedication by congratulating the community for initiating this impressive community development project. Finally, she thanked the UIUC students and faculty. She said, "The Illinois Avenue Playground project is an outstanding example of the urban transformation potential of community/ university partnerships. I look forward to working with local residents and university students and faculty to successfully pursue similar projects in the future."

Marie Drake and James Perry of WIPNO join Ken Reardon in assessing progress being made at the Illinois Avenue Playground construction site (Photo by ESLARP staff)

Following these remarks, the students and faculty boarded several vans for the return trip to campus. Expecting to see everyone in my van asleep within minutes, I was surprised by the animated discussion of lessons learned and future possibilities that our exhausted students engaged in throughout the long ride back to school. The students noted local residents' increasing commitment to the "bottom-up" planning process we had been using. They also highlighted the passion, creativity, and hard work that local children demonstrated throughout the process. While noting the failure of the mayor, city council members, and city manager to make even cameo appearances at the site during the build out, they were eager to build upon the momentum generated by the success of the playground project to undertake larger community development projects using their newly acquired participatory planning and design knowledge and skills.

9. CREATION OF A FARMERS' MARKET

MICHELLE WHETTEN, A FIRST-YEAR GRADUATE student who had worked hard to support the playground project, stopped by my office to tell me that she was interested in preparing a feasibility study and development plan for the farmers' market project that had been featured in both WIPNO's Neighborhood Improvement Plan and its Five-Year Development Strategy.

Professors Andrejasich and Orland expressed strong support for the project, and Michelle indicated that she would prepare a short history of the city's retail food sector to determine when, and under what conditions, local grocery stores had closed. She also planned to complete a literature review focused on the location, form, function and impact of various types of public markets and farmers markets in older industrial cities. Seeking to complete these tasks during the summer, she planned to undertake a small area retail study focused on food stores during the first part of the fall semester to determine if East St. Louis' older residential neighborhoods possessed sufficient purchasing power to support a modest-scale public market or farmers' market. If this research revealed sufficient consumer demand, Michelle said she would conclude her thesis with a preliminary draft of a business plan residents could use to raise funds for this project.

Andrejasich, Orland and I worked together to prepare syllabi for fall classes focused on the potential development of a farmers' market. Orland focused his landscape architecture studio on the development of siting criteria and a preliminary site plan for a city-scale East St. Louis farmers'/public market. He also planned to have his students work with children and teachers from a nearby middle school to design and build a teaching/learning garden for their campus. In the event this school garden produced a surplus, Brian felt these items could be taken to the proposed market for sale. Andrejasich asked his architecture students to visit and analyze the design features of two of the region's most successful farmers'/public markets—St. Louis' historic Soulard Market and the more recently established Kirkwood Farmers' Market. Based upon "best practices" evident at these two facilities, he asked his students to prepare an initial set of designs for improvements needed at such a facility. In addition, he asked them to assess whether a long-abandoned carport on Martin Luther King Jr. Boulevard could serve as the site for an East St. Louis farmers'/public market. Michael also asked his students to prepare construction drawings for several proto-type vender stands that could be inexpensively fabricated by someone without an engineering degree.

Meanwhile, my fall neighborhood planning workshop investigated state and local health ordinances and statutes governing such facilities as well as market rules, application materials, and governance structures used by non-profits and municipal government agencies operating public markets. One of the highlights of our fall studios was a series of field trips we made to the region's most successful markets. During these trips, students created sites plan for each facility; photographed the markets' major physical features; secured copies of their charters, operating rules, application forms, and vender leases and interviewed market managers, long-time merchants, and regular customers. Near the end of the fall semester, Michelle and representatives of our three studios presented the following research findings to WIPNO's Executive Committee.

- With the exception of a few mom and pop groceries, East St. Louis' older residential neighborhoods did not have access to a single full-service grocery store.

- The vast majority of city residents bought most of their groceries in suburban Fairview Heights, Belleville, Collinsville, and the Soulard Market in St. Louis.

- While median incomes within the city's inner city neighborhoods were extremely low, their aggregate purchasing power was sufficient to support a modest scale public market and/or farmers market.

- Area farmers, ranchers, and agricultural producers interested in gaining improved access to the metropolitan St. Louis market appeared willing to participate in an East St. Louis market.

- From the potential merchants' perspective, requirements for the success of such a market were: excellent location, strong security, low-cost structure (i.e. rent and fees), competent management, and aggressive marketing.

- A near ideal location for such a market appeared to be available within the city's Central Business District on Dr. Martin Luther King Jr. Boulevard.

- The University of Illinois and University of Missouri Cooperative Extension Services were willing to assist WIPNO in recruiting farmers, ranchers, and fish farmers to provide products at an East. St. Louis market.

- Considerable community support existed for the development of a seasonal farmers market that would be reasonably inexpensive and quick to launch demonstrating the existence of a robust consumer market for healthy foods in East St. Louis.

WIPNO's leaders were impressed by the students' research and fully supportive of the development of a seasonal farmers market at the site of the former used-car dealership. They approved the report and a related proposal to establish a joint WIPNO/UIUC Farmers' Market Planning Committee that Michelle and other students agreed to staff.

Over the 1993-94 holidays these students, guided by Professors Andrejasich, Orland, Selby and I, formulated a detailed work plan to secure site control and prepare an architectural program for the market. The plan proposed completion of architectural and construction drawings by February; launch of a fundraising campaign by March; recruitment of regional farmers, producers and construction volunteers by April; and organization of a "Grand Opening" of the East St. Louis Farmers Market by early May.

By the time the spring 1994 semester began, ESLARP's graduate research assistants and faculty (with the assistance of township supervisor McGaughey, Bill Kreeb of the Neighborhood House, and Rep. Younge) had secured site control of the site and finalized the architectural program for its transformation. Students enrolled in my neighborhood planning workshop and in architectural studios with Andrejasich and Selby found themselves "volunteered" for a number of East St. Louis service days to remove trash, fill holes in parking areas and paint the carport. They were also given the opportunity to work on the following activities:

- Development of information packets to be used by Illinois and Missouri Cooperative Extension Service staff in recruiting would-be merchants.

- Creation of an attractive East St. Louis logo, branding statement, and visual presentation materials.

- Design and construction of 30 8' by 4' vender tables that were easy to set up, flexible for use with different products, collapsible for storage, and relatively inexpensive.

- Completion of a comprehensive architectural program for the building and site transforming them into an exciting retail shopping and cultural/arts venue.

- Creation of a plan to use approximately half of the site as a communal gardening area to introduce residents to raised-bed cultivation techniques that could generate additional products for sale in the market.

- Organization of a daylong training program to introduce would-be merchants to the organization, operation, opportunities, and challenges of conducting a successful business in an urban farmers' market.

- Generation of market rules, leasing agreements, and a rent schedule to be used in operating the market.

- Organization of a "kick-off" event and a series of promotional activities to encourage East St. Louis families and institutions to shop at the market.

More than 100 UIUC students worked together to complete this list of tasks before the East St. Louis Farmers' Market's official opening on Saturday, May 7, 1994. We quickly learned that the physical transformation of the site was not the most challenging aspect of the project: rather, it was the effort needed to convince a critical mass of regional farmers to bring the "fruits of their labor" and their equipment to the heart of an African-American city that had been regularly described by journalists as beyond redemption. In order to overcome the "taken for granted" assumptions that many farmers had, that East St. Louis was simply not safe, ESLARP had to take a number of unusual steps.

Working with experienced extension agents from both Illinois and Missouri, we did a mailing to regional farmers and producers that included a cover letter, program brochure, site plan, and photos of the facility. ESLARP students then called each farmer and producer in order to gauge their interest in the market offering to visit the farms or ranches of those intrigued by the development to provide additional information regarding the facility. WIPNO also hosted an "open house" for interested farmers and ranchers at Rev. Wilson's church. Following a short prayer and a slideshow highlighting the impressive list of community development projects completed by ESLARP and its neighborhood partners, six area farmers boarded a UIUC van to visit the farmers' market site where they found dozens of community and campus volunteers working hard to transform an old carport into an attractive retail food store. The visiting farmers readily admitted being nervous about doing business in downtown East St. Louis, however, they also shared their excitement about joining a community/university partnership committed to building a very unique farmers' market. A few days after our meeting and tour all but two of the visiting farmers signaled their commitment to the effort by sending their signed leases and seasonal rental payments to WIPNO.

We raised the funds needed to transform the site and its existing structure into an attractive public market space through donations from many of the same individuals and firms who had contributed to the Illinois Avenue Playground project. Professors Orland, Andrejasich, Selby and I, organized a series of work weekends in late March and April to create what we described as a "drop dead beautiful market." The work began with the tedious and exhausting removal of two dumpsters worth of trash and building debris from the site. The landscape architecture students then constructed raised flowerbeds that dramatically improved the site's appearance. A second section of raised beds for locally grown fruits and vegetables were to serve as teaching plots that also separated the site's large parking area from its food sales and public performance spaces.

Architecture students were busy fixing minor leaks in the roof of the carport, and building a large storage room, market manager's office and public bathrooms with the assistance of James Perry, a former firefighter turned contractor. Excitement regarding the successful completion of these spaces was short-lived when the site, including these new enclosures, quickly flooded from a combination of rain water and sewage. Kirk Goodrich, one of our assistants whose father was a Brooklyn plumbing contractor, began digging to identify the source of our drainage problem. Attempting to assist Kirk, I dug a bit too enthusiastically around the source of the leak exacerbating the original fracture and causing the trench that Kirk and I were standing in to quickly fill with additional effluent that soon came up to our waists. This evoked howls of laughter and non-stop ribbing from my colleagues regarding the importance of skilled labor in the building process.

Rev. Watson of WIPNO and Kirk Goodrich, a former ESLARP graduate research assistant and WIPNO's first Executive Director, at the future site of the East St. Louis Farmers' Market (Photo by K. Reardon).

Following a costly repair of the sewer line, our planning students coordinated the efforts of community and campus volunteers to power wash, sand, and paint the interior and exterior of the carport. As this work began, four young boys from the neighborhood appeared at the site eager to help. We ultimately gave them a small scaffold from which they could easily and safely paint the lower portion of the structure. Seeking to avoid any chance of them ruining their clothes or hurting themselves, we gave them several oversized East St. Louis Farmers' Market t-shirts, protective eyewear, and work gloves to wear. Everything appeared to be going well until I caught the scaffolding swaying wildly. Bored by the seemingly endless nature of the painting task they decided to play "chicken" on the structure rocking it from side to side to see who would be the last person to jump off. Unfortunately, they had left their paint buckets on hooks near the top of the structure. As the scaffolding tipped over, all four of them quickly abandoned the structure, but not before a healthy volume of white paint had spilled on their heads and shoulders. When they pealed their goggles off, everyone roared with laughter. These four African-American boys were now as white as snow with the exception of the areas around their eyes that had been protected by their goggles prompting Kirk to say that they resembled baby raccoons.

A group of planning students painted wide vertical stripes evocative of West African Kinta cloth along the angled (mansard-like) roof that ran the entire length of the carport facing Dr. Martin Luther King Jr. Boulevard giving the structure a dramatic new "signature" feature. Don Johnson and Pat Brown, two graduate architecture students assisted a local contractor in installing new lighting, overhead fans, and additional electrical outlets throughout the market. In addition, they designed, fabricated and installed wire and pipe fixtures at the market's four entranceways that were used to display beautifully designed, "Welcome to the East St. Louis Farmers' Market" banners. Complimenting these interior signs and the facade was a large rooftop sign that Jim Hanley, one of our assistant's brothers, a skilled metal fabricator, custom made for the market. This beautifully rendered eight-by-three foot sign, when lit, was clearly visible for several blocks along MLK Boulevard.

The final improvement made to the former carport was the installation of more than two dozen vender booths that could be easily installed, anchored to the market floor throughout the season, and collapsed for winter storage. Students enrolled in Prof. Andrejasich's Architecture 100 class designed these. WIPNO leaders reviewed their work and chose a design where the display surface could be tilted to show fruits and vegetable, left flat to display baked goods and fresh flowers using circular openings in the surface.

The weekend before the market opened nearly two dozen architecture students travelled to East St. Louis with a Ryder truck filled with lumber, hardware, and tools. Over a two-day period, these students constructed twenty-eight vender stands while completing various other improvements contained on the project's final construction "punch list." The addition of the vender stands; flowers and shrubs, interior and exterior signage, and the grand opening banner generated considerable excitement among residents who had been carefully monitoring the project's progress.

A group of eleven merchants participated in a two-day training program designed to help them to succeed in the challenging retail food sector. The program, was designed by Roger Sexton, a graduate planning student and myself, and included topics such as: product selection, pricing, and display; market rules and regulations; health department inspections and food handling rules; basic business accounting; point of sale merchandising and customer relations. Among the eleven individuals were five area farmers, the majority of whom had never participated in an urban farmers' market before, and six East St. Louis residents who planned to pool their resources to buy fruits and vegetables, at wholesale prices at St. Louis Soulard Market, for resale at retail prices at the East St. Louis Farmers' Market. Many farmers' markets reject "wholesale to retail" venders, however WIPNO's Executive Committee believed it was more important to bring wholesome foods into the city—regardless of their source—than to restrict supply to those farmers and producers operating in the immediate (less than 250 miles) vicinity. The last prospective merchant was Bessie Spencer, a long-time East St. Louis schoolteacher, who sought to augment her modest Social Security benefits and teacher's pension with income from the sale of what she described as "passion greens"—a type of collard green that offered a bit of kick.

As the market's opening day approached, ESLARP issued a series of press releases describing the launch of the city's first new retail food outlet in more than twenty-five years. Students visited area churches, schools, cultural/recreational centers, and senior citizen facilities to encourage people to attend the market's formal opening. ESLARP also hired an army of high school students to distribute flyers to local residents and business owners throughout the Emerson Park, Lansdowne, Winstanley/Industry Park, Olivette Park, Edgemont, Alta Sita and South End neighborhoods.

As these activities were taking place, Prof. Lew Hopkins and I visited the newly appointed associate director of UIUC's Cooperative Extension Service, John Van Es, to update him on the progress being made in East St. Louis and to invite his unit to become more engaged in this effort. Hopkins described how our efforts might assist Cooperative Extension in addressing a critical challenge facing their system—the state and nation's dramatic shift from a rural to urban society.

Lew, who was a long-time extension supporter, said he believed the institution's future depended, in large part, on its ability to promote creative solutions to the development challenges facing urban and suburban communities. Lew argued the agency needed to complement its existing staff, (overwhelming white and focused on rural development) with people of color who possessed the knowledge and skills to resolve challenging urban problems. Lew asked John Van Es to consider allocating two entry-level extension educator positions to ESLARP where an interdisciplinary faculty would recruit African-American and Latino graduates in architecture, landscape architecture, and urban planning to fill these positions. Subsequent to their appointments these minority professionals would work with ESLARP faculty to acquire the skills needed to manage highly participatory community planning processes increasingly in demand in urban areas throughout the state. Lew suggested a two-year period of service for these new extension educators during which time they would collaborate with the leadership of East St. Louis growing citizen planning movement on a series of increasingly challenging development projects. After this, these young professionals would be available to initiate university-supported urban revitalization projects in other cities served by extension. We were delighted when Associate Director Van Es responded favorably to Lew's proposal indicating that he hoped we could recruit, screen, and hire the first of our two urban extension educators by the following fall.

On Saturday, May 7, 1994, more than 150 East St. Louis residents, business owners, and elected officials were joined by more than thirty ESLARP volunteers to celebrate the opening of the East St. Louis Farmers' Market. Following a short invocation by Rev. Herman Watson, Kirk Goodrich, who served as the MC for the dedication, introduced Carol Perry, WIPNO's President, who described how Michelle Whetten's capstone project and approximately 15,000 hours of volunteer labor by local residents and UIUC students had transformed this long-abandoned used car lot into an attractive retail market and civic space. Rep. Younge described the impact the facility was already having on nearby commercial property owners who were renewing their efforts to improve the area. The day's last speaker was East St. Louis' newly elected mayor, Gordon Bush, who described the successful development of the market as a powerful example of the "New East St. Louis." At the conclusion of the formal program, Kirk asked everyone present to join him in counting down to the opening of the market. He then invited the crowd to let go of the helium filled balloons they had been given which read—"East St. Louis Farmers' Market—OPEN FOR BUSINESS!" at the end of their countdown. Rev. James Cowan, a long-time East St. Louis minister in his mid-80's was asked to come forward to cut the ribbon marking the facility's formal opening.

For the next five years, six to eight merchants regularly rented between fifteen to twenty vendor stands at the farmers market offering a wide assortment of fresh fruits, vegetables, breads, cakes, and pies. One of the most exciting and unexpected developments that took place shortly after the market's opening was when a local farmer, at his own expense brought refrigerated display cases to the site from which he sold beef, poultry, pork, eggs, and cheese products. Between 1994 and 1999, the East St. Louis Farmers' Market functioned as one of the only sources of fresh food within East St. Louis' central business district doing approximately $50,000 and $75,000 in annual sales. In addition to providing low-income residents easy access to healthy foods, the market served as an important civic and cultural space. Under WIPNO's management, the East St. Louis Farmers' Market served as a venue for school bands, dance troupes, and step groups. It was also the site for many food preparation, presentation and storage demonstrations by UIUC's Cooperative Extension staff. The market had quickly become an important retail and cultural center.

Local church choir sing freedom songs at the ESL Farmers' Market during lunch at the 1995 Planners Network Conference (Photo by K. Reardon).

10. OLIVETTE PARK AND BACKLASH FROM THE POLITICAL MACHINE

THE SUCCESS OF THE PLAYGROUND and farmers' market projects, along with the ongoing home repairs that students continued to undertake in other neighborhoods, strengthened the bonds among the city's community leaders and UIUC's students and faculty. As work on the market approached its final phase, the faculty advisory committee was invited to meet with Lamar Gentry, East St. Louis' City Manager, executives from Community Development Associates, a St. Louis-based firm responsible for operating the city's Community Development Block Grant Program and Diane Bonner, the newly-appointed acting director of this program. Lamar Gentry, Diane Bonner, and Lou Berra, president of the Community Development Associates, invited ESLARP to respond to an upcoming RFP for comprehensive planning services in the Olivette Park neighborhood located just west of the Winstanley/Industry Park community where we were then working.

Leaders of this neighborhood had recently lobbied the city to get ESLARP to initiate a community planning effort in their neighborhood similar to the one we had recently completed in the Winstanley/Industry Park community. These individuals appeared convinced that the kind of planning we were pursuing in Winstanley/Industry Park had the potential to significantly improve conditions in their neighborhood, once called "Society Hill" because of the number of local elites who lived there. They also believed such an effort could further stimulate further beautification and commercial investment along an important section of MLK Blvd located within the city's central business district.

ESLARP faculty discussed the challenges of maintaining planning and development activities in four separate neighborhoods, but decided to recruit a small group of graduate planning students to prepare a response to the city's RFP. Angie Morgan Marks, Patricia Nolan, and Eric Stoller—second-year graduate planning students—

worked with Professors Andrejasich, Orland, Selby, and myself to prepare our submission. When we encountered language within the RFP requiring the consultants to give special attention to the neighborhood's cultural assets, we invited Professors Bruce Wicks and Cary McDonald of UIUC's Department of Recreation, Sports, and Tourism to join us on our submission and, in the event we were awarded this contract, to collaborate in preparing what would be ESLARP's first integrated comprehensive revitalization plan and cultural district development strategy. The addition of Professors Wicks and McDonald enabled us to integrate students and faculty from a fourth UIUC school, the College of Applied Life Sciences, into a project that had already involved the Colleges of Fine and Applied Arts, Arts and Sciences, and Law.

As the end of the summer of 1995 approached, Weeks and I organized graduate students from urban planning and from recreation, sports and tourism to create a work plan designed to produce a comprehensive plan and cultural development strategy in the event we received the contract. Near the beginning of the fall semester of 1995, the city informed us that they had decided to fund ESLARP's proposal to provide planning services for the Olivette Park community. I was especially pleased when the three graduate planning students who had assisted the faculty in drafting the project's preliminary work plan subsequently agreed to work together to produce the Olivette Park Neighborhood Revitalization Plan under the department's newly established "group capstone" option. This option had been developed to accommodate students' desires to work on larger-scale planning and design projects, such as this one, in East St. Louis. As the fall semester of 1995 began, Angie Morgan Marks, Patricia Nolan, and Eric Stoller assisted by Rep. Younge, township supervisor McGaughey, Bill Kreeb of Neighborhood House, and Joe Hubbard of Catholic Urban Programs formed a steering committee, as we had done in the Emerson Park, Lansdowne, and Winstanley/Industry Park neighborhoods, to provide direction to this exciting new initiative.

Aware of the need to involve a broader range of community interests on the steering committee, the students tried unsuccessfully to elicit the Olivette Park Local Development Corporation's help in forming a more representative advisory body. When this effort failed, the students convinced the leaders of the newly organized Olivette Park Neighborhood Association, led by Mamie Bolden and Rocco Goins, to assist them in mobilizing local block clubs, tenant associations, senior citizen organizations, churches, small business, and human service organizations to participate in the planning process.

Under the leadership of this newly-expanded steering committee, these students, assisted by volunteers enrolled in "Introduction to City and Regional Planning" that I taught, successfully collected and analyzed the key data needed to prepare an empirically-based comprehensive plan for this historic African-American neighborhood. Among the data they examined were past Olivette Park studies, reports, and plans; recent population, employment, income/poverty and housing trends and projections; community assets and resources inventories, and local ownership, property values, and tax arrearages/foreclosures trends. The students also collected and analyzed land use, building conditions, and property maintenance surveys; local infrastructure inventories and assessments; and, local residents and institutional leaders' revitalization preferences. Finally the students reviewed national "best practices" in resident-led, arts-based community stabilization and revitalization. Local stakeholders joined UIUC students and faculty in evaluating the policy implications of these and other data using the participatory planning process created and refined during our Emerson Park, Lansdowne, and Winstanley/Industry Park planning efforts.

As ESLARP's planning students engaged in the data collection/ analysis, goal setting, and plan development phases of the Olivette Park planning process in the winter of 1995 and the spring of 1996, Professors Wicks and McDonald and their students were busy identifying, mapping, and analyzing the neighborhood's artistic and cultural resources. They gave special attention to gaps in the local service delivery system for arts and cultural programming, areas of overlapping and/or redundant services, and unrealized opportunities for cooperative arts programs involving local schools, colleges, universities, park districts, museums, and non-profit arts organizations.

Data collected by the team as part of this process identified the following eleven factors as Olivette Park's most important assets/resources:

1. Central location with easy access to many of the city, county and region's most important educational, health care, cultural and business centers;

2. Proximity to I-55/70 and 64 offering neighborhood residents and businesses excellent access to resources in the balance of Illinois as well as nearby Missouri;

3. A mixed land use pattern providing local residents, businesses, and institutions convenient access to a wide range of goods and services;

4. A significant number of vacant building parcels, owned by the county, that have excellent adaptive re-use potential;

5. A building stock that had held up very well despite decades of "redlining" by local financial institutions and greenlining by local governmental agencies;

6. The presence of a number of community-based arts programs serving "at risk" youth, especially the Katherine Dunham Centers for Arts and Humanities;

7. The existence of several successful African-American businesses with deep commitments to expanding economic and community development opportunities for local residents and businesspersons;

8. The presence of nineteen religious institutions offering a wide range of educational, recreational, cultural, health/nutrition, and pastoral services; fifteen of which were involved in the Olivette Park revitalization planning process;

9. A high level of resident participation in civic affairs encouraged by an active network of tenant associations, homeowners' organizations, fraternal societies and arts groups;

10. A rich social history based upon the neighborhood's popularity among the city's local elites. Among those who had called Olivette Park home were the legendary jazz musician, Miles Davis, and the anthropologist, dancer, choreographer, educator, artist, and humanitarian Katherine Dunham; and,

11. The city's recent rediscovery of and commitment to Olivette Park as evidenced by its funding of several major street improvements and community service facilities in the neighborhood, including the East St. Louis Public Library and the Lessie Bates Davis Family Development Center.

The residents involved in the creation of the Olivette Park Revitalization Plan sought to address low educational attainment, unemployment, poverty, crime, infrastructure failures, housing deterioration and population and business losses confronting their neighborhood by crafting a comprehensive plan that capitalized, in a strategic manner, on their abovementioned assets. The planning process culminated with the first annual Olivette Park neighborhood summit that more than eighty stakeholders attended in May of 1996.

The summit identified the following overall development goal: To utilize Olivette Park's significant physical, social, spiritual and human resources to improve the quality of life for residents and business owners through a comprehensive community development strategy featuring environmental restoration, crime prevention, housing improvement, business development and expansion and arts programming.

With the assistance of more than a dozen community development specialists, recruited by ESLARP, local stakeholders identified the following six community development objectives to guide their future neighborhood stabilization and revitalization activities:

1. To enhance the residential quality of Olivette Park by preserving and improving the neighborhood's existing housing stock as well as finding opportunities to produce new affordable housing.

2. To improve the health and safety of all residents as well as the appearance of the neighborhood through a series of environmental restoration programs and activities.

3. To strengthen public safety in Olivette Park through the development of a crime prevention and home and business security program.

4. To expand local businesses and employment by informing residents and business owners of available resources,

providing unemployed and underemployed residents with job skills to improve their job prospects and creating a business environment that fosters local entrepreneurship.

5. To use the neighborhood's considerable cultural and historic assets to promote the revitalization of its physical environment and to strengthen its social fabric.

6. To increase educational, recreational, and cultural opportunities for local youth by encouraging their participation and commitment to the neighborhood's redevelopment.

At the Olivette Park neighborhood summit, participants identified thirty-one immediate, intermediate, and long-term improvement projects. Critical to the success of these initiatives would be the ongoing development of the Olivette Park Neighborhood Association's organizational capacity. The plan's extensive implementation section focused on proposals to transform this small but effective neighborhood association into a fully developed community development corporation—one capable of raising significant external funding to support the plan's more ambitious economic and community development projects.

The organizational capacity section of the plan featured a series of initiatives to expand the organization's membership base; identify and train new leaders, especially among the neighborhood's many young adults; develop a more ample and diversified funding base; and recruit, train, and supervise a small staff of community development professionals to support the self-help efforts of local residents and leaders. This section concluded with a discussion of the local, state, and national affiliations the neighborhood association should establish to secure the external funding and technical assistance needed to implement the plan's most complex projects.

Olivette Park residents and leaders, especially it's leading businesspersons and pastors, were enthusiastic supporters of the plan. Shortly after stakeholders at the Summit adopted the plan, city officials invited the neighborhood association to apply for $50,000 in CDBG funding to initiate several of the neighborhood plan's immediate and intermediate-term beautification, home repair, and community-based arts projects. When the Association's receipt of a $50,000

CDBG grant from the City was reported in the local press, officers of the Olivette Park Neighborhood Association and ESLARP faculty were invited to meet with Mayor Gordon Bush. When our delegation arrived at his several days later, we found Mayor Bush, the director of a local business association, and a religious leader. Following an exchange of pleasantries, the Mayor stated that he had only recently learned about the neighborhood association's grant. After congratulating our team on the success of our application, he encouraged us to consider using the long-established Olivette Park Local Development Corporation as our fiscal agent in light of their experience managing such funding. Both of the community leaders attending the meeting were board members of the Olivette Park Local Development Corporation who explained the benefits of using an established 501c3 as an intermediary on our first major grant and the relatively modest costs associated in doing so.

I explained that we had already made arrangements with the Katherine Dunham Centers for Arts and Humanities to serve as the fiscal agent for our grant. After thanking these leaders for their generous offer to serve as our fiscal agent, I told them that we could not imagine having a better fiscal agent for our grant, the majority of which was going to fund arts programming for children, than Katherine Dunham who had been one of the very first recipients of the Kennedy Center's Lifetime Achievement Award as well as a U.S. State Department's Cultural Ambassador-at-Large to Africa. When these representatives raised the non-resident nature of Dunham's board, I asked them how many members of the Olivette Park Local Development Corporation's Board were current residents of Olivette Park.

Frustrated by our refusal to run our first neighborhood planning grant through the Olivette Park Local Development Corporation, these individuals predicted serious implementation problems if we failed to heed their "fiscal agent" advice. They highlighted their concerns by emphasizing our lack of experience managing government grants and mentioning the probationary or temporary nature of my university employment since I was in the final year of my probationary period for promotion and tenure at UIUC.

One of the development corporation representatives asked, "What impact would charges of discriminatory planning and practices by ESLARP and the Olivette Park Neighborhood Association have upon the long-term success of your East St. Louis efforts?" I responded by inviting the mayor to ask Katherine Dunham what she thought of the development corporation's proposal to make their organization, that had never received and administered a major arts award, the fiscal agent for this grant, rather than her organization. I went on to say that if Dunham was prepared to approve this change than we would enthusiastically support it. Without her support, however, we were unwilling to accept the development corporation's offer to manage our grant for a fee, an offer made with a not so subtle political threat which I viewed as nothing less than extortion.

When the Olivette Park Neighborhood Association and ESLARP subsequently reaffirmed its commitment to using the Katherine Dunham Centers for Arts and Humanities as its fiscal agent for the grant, Ishaq Shafiq, who was then serving as Mayor Bush's chief of staff, warned us that we were courting political disaster by not agreeing to the development corporation's request. Eager to initiate work on the neighborhood beautification, community arts, and housing preservation projects identified as immediate-term projects in the Olivette Park Neighborhood Revitalization Plan, and unwilling to pay what I regarded as an "extortion fee," I decided to ignore this warning from my former graduate assistant.

In less than six months, the ESLARP faculty was invited to the UIUC Chancellor's office where we were informed that the Illinois Legislative Black Caucus had unanimously passed a resolution condemning ESLARP as a racist organization that was using state funds to pursue policies designed to silence the voices of indigenous African-American leaders to perpetuate uneven patterns of metropolitan development responsible for persistent poverty in East St. Louis. We were informed by the Vice-Chancellor for Affirmative Action and Diversity that a formal complaint accusing me of racially discriminatory practices had been filed. My appearance was required before a university-wide tribunal that would take place before faculty in my department and college would be considering my promotion and tenure.

The Vice-Chancellor shared copies of the Illinois Legislative Black Caucus' resolution as well as their formal complaint against me. While the resolution might cause a certain amount of public relations concern among university administrators, the formal complaint could, in fact, have caused me to be formally sanctioned and/or terminated as a probationary UIUC faculty member. As a result, I was much more concerned about the formal complaint that charged me with a long list of discriminatory practices during the recently complete Olivette Park planning process, including:

1. Failure to invite representatives of local African-American civic, fraternal, professional and civil rights organizations to participate in the Olivette Park planning process.

2. Refusal to include representatives from these organizations on the steering committee for an Olivette Park Neighborhood Revitalization Plan.

3. Denial of the rights of such organizational representatives to speak at the sub-committee meetings, neighborhood assemblies, and community summit at which times the content of the Olivette Park Neighborhood Revitalization Plan was formulated.

4. Exclusion of such organizations from consideration as grantees and sub-contractors under externally funded grants secured during the implementation phase of the Olivette Park Neighborhood Revitalization Plan.

While my administratively and politically-astute department head, Lew Hopkins, was telling me not to worry about the complaint; the Vice-Chancellor, who attended the meeting and would be chairing the panel that would hear this complaint, described these as serious charges that needed to be refuted if we are "to clear your good name." After reviewing the specific charges alleged in the complaint, the students who had worked on the plan and I were confident that we possessed overwhelming evidence to refute charges.

Before leaving the meeting, Angie Morgan Marks, Patricia Nolan, and Eric Stoller, who had served as our graduate research assistants for the Olivette Park Neighborhood Revitalization Plan, had already begun identifying the evidence we had to address the charges contained in the complaint. Disregarding Professor Hopkins advice to not mount a "Clarence Darrow-like defense," the students and I prepared a long memo responding to the primary charge of systematic exclusion of local African-American leaders from meaningful participation in the Olivette Park planning process.

This response was possible, in large part, due to the systematic approach these students had taken to ensure that the resident-led planning process in Olivette Park reflected the hopes and aspirations of local stakeholders. Among the most compelling evidence my students and I gathered to document the inclusionary and democratic nature of the Olivette Park planning process were the following items:

1. A comprehensive list of more than fifty African-American resident, business, labor, fraternal, religious, professional, political, and human service organizations that had been regularly invited to participate in the Olivette Park planning process.

2. A comprehensive list of the more than 600 local residents, business owners, and institutional leaders, nearly all of whom were people of color, who had attended one or more of the community meetings that had taken place during the planning process. The names of nearly all of the individuals who had signed the formal complaint against me appeared on these sign-in sheets.

3. A list of more than forty local leaders, with their organizational affiliations, with whom we had conducted one-on-one interviews in order to elicit their perceptions and views of current community conditions as well as their preferred redevelopment scenarios.

4. A tally of the number of local heads of households we had surveyed during our door-to-door resident interviews to elicit their views of current conditions and preferred redevelopment strategies. Again, nearly all of those we had signed the complaint against me had been interviewed.

5. A reflective essay identifying the multiple community sources that were the inspiration for each of the immediate, intermediate, and long-term community development projects featured in the Olivette Park Neighborhood Revitalization Plan.

6. A review of the local affiliations of each member of the steering committee for an Olivette Park Neighborhood Revitalization Plan that documented their deep roots within the city's African-American community.

In addition to our extended brief we had a series of video clips from our planning meetings in which the very individuals who were charging me with "denying people of color their voice" were shown addressing these forums.

As the hearing date approached, I received a call from Jeanelle Stovall, special assistant to Katherine Dunham, who explained that she had recently heard about my predicament. Stovall explained Dunham's desire to provide a strong letter of support for ESLARP's and my work in Olivette Park. I was deeply touched by Dunham's willingness to "go to bat" for us and said that we would welcome a letter from her to the Vice-Chancellor.

A few weeks later, Professor Hopkins, my students, and I sat in a conference room in the UIUC Administration building waiting for the formal hearing on my discrimination complaint to begin. The session started with the Vice-Chancellor reading the Olivette Park Local Development Corporation's complaint against me. He then asked me to review the highlights of my brief for the hearing panel that was composed of several campus deans. As I was about to begin my refutation of the Olivette Park Local Development Corporation's charges, one of the deans on the panel raised a "point of order." He explained that the panel, as a quasi-judicial body with the power to recommend sanctions against me, had the responsibility to ensure that those bringing charges had made a strong *prima facie* case of actual wrongdoing before asking me to defend myself. In his opinion, the Olivette Park Local Development Corporation had failed to provide concrete evidence that I had excluded anyone from participating in the Olivette Park planning process. He concluded his remarks by chiding the Vice-Chancellor, who was presiding over the hearing for stating in his opening remarks his desire to see "my good name cleared of these charges." The dean stated, "We do Prof. Reardon and his colleagues a disservice by stating our hopes to exonerate them from charges that have been offered without any empirical proof."

Noting his procedural concern, which the other two deans on

the panel appeared to share, the Vice Chancellor invited me respond to the charges. For the next thirty minutes, I reviewed the specific charges contained in the Olivette Park Local Development Corporation's letter of complaint using the data contained in our brief. I concluded my remarks by showing clips of several of those who had charged me with denying them and other people of color "voice" within a publicly sponsored and funded community planning process addressing the Olivette Park neighborhood summit at which the programmatic content of the Neighborhood Revitalization Plan was formulated with the participation of more than eighty neighborhood stakeholders. In doing so, I made a special effort to show that many of the recommendations offered by my accusers during the video clips had been incorporated into the final draft of the Olivette Park Neighborhood Revitalization Plan.

Following my remarks, the Vice-Chancellor invited the deans participating on the review panel to ask me any questions they might have. At this point, one of the deans asked me why I thought a small but influential group of local leaders had chosen to file a formal complaint against a project that, on the surface, appeared to be "doing everything right." I explained how the eighty-year old political machine controlling East St. Louis had created conditions under which any individual and/or organization seeking to implement a significant economic and/or community development project requiring city regulatory approval or financial support was expected to provide "benefits" to their allies either in the form of jobs and contracts. I explained how we were working with local leaders committed to challenging such corrupt practices in hopes of reestablishing democratic governance in this community explaining that we could not help them achieve this goal if we participated in local political patronage.

Before proceeding to the hearing's deliberation phase the Vice-Chancellor said he had received a letter from a significant African-American leader within the community who had participated in the Olivette Park planning process. He then read excerpts from a handwritten letter from Katherine Dunham praising our work and characterizing those who had lodged the complaint against us as little better than petty thieves. She concluded her letter by saying that our work deserved nothing less than the university's full support.

At this point, one of the deans on the panel offered a resolution rejecting the Olivette Park Local Development Corporation's charges based upon their failure to provide evidence supporting these claims and the Olivette Park planning team's extensive documentation of the highly participatory and inclusive nature of our planning process. Within minutes the other deans on the review panel voiced their support of this resolution. The Vice-Chancellor conducting the hearing indicated he would inform those who had lodged the complaint that a thorough review of the charges had been conducted by an independent body at UIUC that cleared myself and ESLARP of these charges.

Leaving the hearing, my students and I shared our relief in having survived a potentially deadly political challenge. We also shared our deep disappointment that Rep. Younge, whom we had worked with for so long, had co-sponsored the Illinois Legislative Black Caucus's resolution citing our work as examples of unexamined white privilege and academic colonialism. Her public support of those attacking us, despite our close cooperation with her office, helped us appreciate the delicate position of local reformers. As much as she admired the participatory planning work we were doing in the city's poorest neighborhoods, her reelection still depended on the support of the East St. Louis and St. Clair County Democratic organizations. In the absence of a broad-based citizen movement for municipal reform, officials such as Rep. Younge would be forced to "throw us under the bus," regardless of their respect for us if our activities threatened their political allies.

This close call in Olivette Park made us critically aware of three things. First, our efforts to empower the city's poor and working-class families were being increasingly viewed as a threat to the local political machine. Second, public support from influential African-American leaders, such as Dunham, was essential to our long-term political survival within the city. Third, we had to scrupulously document our methods and findings to be able to defend ourselves against future charges that would most certainly come.

11. ENHANCING OUR COMMUNITY PLANNING, DESIGN AND DEVELOPMENT CAPACITY

AS THE NUMBER OF NEIGHBORHOODS where ESLARP was engaged in planning, design, and development activities grew, the project needed to enhance its organizational capacity. Fortunately, core faculty had the ability to continually adapt their research, teaching, and outreach approach in response to changing community conditions that often did not respond to mainstream planning and design solutions.

The faculty were unusually adept experiential learners, as described by David Kolb. We initially used mainstream urban planning, urban design, and community change principles and techniques to develop "orienting theories" that shaped our expectations regarding how various East St. Louis practice settings might function and to provide guidance regarding how to best approach our work. Using these orienting theories, we inventoried the planning problems at hand, identified those requiring immediate attention, and framed these for future action. We subsequently used these theories to carry out specific community improvements aimed at enhancing the overall quality of life in the neighborhoods where we were working during what Kolb describes as the "concrete experience" phase of the experiential learning cycle. Following this step, we evaluated discrepancies arising between what our orienting theories suggested the intervention outcomes should accomplish and the actual outcomes we achieved, during what Kolb labeled the "systematic reflection" phase of the experiential learning cycle. Examining these differences between our theoretical expectations and actual experiences, we then formulated new improvement strategies based upon the integration of these two forms of knowing testing these new understandings in the often-messy world of East St. Louis practice during what Kolb identified as the "active experimentation" phase of the experiential learning cycle.

During ESLARP's first decade we repeatedly followed this cyclical process to strengthen our ability to support the city's increasingly active resident-led planning and development movement and to maximize our students' learning outcomes. Some faculty referred to our approach using Argryis, Smith, and Putnam's action science, Shon's reflective practice, Forester's deliberative practice, and Greenwood and Levin's participatory action research terminology.

Our work was characterized by a common commitment to:

- Working on problems identified by residents living and working in East St. Louis' most distressed neighborhoods.

- Involving the residents most affected by the problems being addressed as co-investigators, with researchers and professionals, at each step in the planning process.

- Pursuing the investigation of these issues using a reciprocal learning process in which the local knowledge of area stakeholders was integrated with the expert knowledge of professionals to achieve deeper insights into the problems at hand and consideration of a wider range of potential intervention strategies.

- Testing these new community transformation ideas by using them to forge action strategies, policies, plans, and projects designed to affect positive change.

- Reflecting upon the effectiveness of these theories by critically evaluating the quality of life outcomes these interventions produced.

- Applying Saul Alinsky's "Golden Rule" of community organization by consistently challenging local residents and leaders to assume responsibility for initiating and maintaining community problem-solving, planning, design, development, and management activities.

What explains the faculty's willingness and ability to continually re-evaluate, reframe and redirect their activities, frequently adopting practices that many viewed as unconventional and in some cases radical? ESLARP's founding faculty came from families in which strong religious beliefs produced a deep commitment to social justice. When mainstream planning and design approaches failed to address the needs of our East St. Louis neighbors my colleagues and I were simply unwilling to walk away. In addition, the original ESLARP faculty had significant professional experience in architecture, landscape architecture, city planning and community organization prior to entering the academy. Each was willing to return to our previous professional roles, if and when, the university no longer provided what E.P. Thompson called a "steepled place" for democratic, and even seditious, talk and action. Also, the project's location nearly 200 miles from our campus sheltered ESLARP students and faculty from many of the institutional concerns and conservative tendencies of university administrators. Finally, the failure of the UIUC's previous community development work in East St. Louis and several other African-American communities in Illinois had become a public embarrassment and legislative problem for the institution. The ESLARP faculty felt pressure from community residents, area officials, and university administrators to make something happen in East St. Louis which gave them the psychological freedom and political license to take poet Robert Frost's "road less travelled."

During the project's first ten years of existence, ESLARP students and faculty generated a number of what William F. Whyte described as "social inventions for human problem-solving" to enhance our ability to support resident-led redevelopment in East St. Louis. Among the most significant of these changes were the following:

REBRANDING OF THE PROJECT: A cross-section of local leaders, who had participated in or closely observed UIUC's Urban Extension and Minority Access Project (UEMAP) felt it was another example of the university using the city as an urban laboratory where faculty and students could use "strip mining" data collection techniques to advance their scholarly publishing and external fundraising efforts, with little regard for community impacts. Participating faculty felt the need to shift to a less exploitative approach to community research that would provide significant mutual benefits for community and campus partners. In 1991, my colleagues and I decided to embrace a participatory action research approach to our East St. Louis work, move from semester length to multi-year projects, and drop the Urban Extension and Minority Access Project name in favor of the East St. Louis Action Research Project (ESLARP). This rebranding emphasized our commitment to resident-led change, democratic planning and design, and citizen empowerment.

A MULTI-DISCIPLINARY APPROACH: In 1991, I invited several of the architecture and landscape architecture faculty who had been engaged in individual community-based research projects in East St. Louis and elsewhere, to join me in designing and offering an interdisciplinary summer program on "place-making" in East St. Louis that culminated in a field-based planning project in the Lansdowne neighborhood. The transformational learning experiences students and faculty gained while engaging in this interdisciplinary field-based research project prompted us to propose the integration of what, to date, had been independent community-based planning efforts by the School of Architecture and the Departments of City and Regional Planning and Landscape Architecture. In 1991, a faculty advisory committee for the newly integrated project was established and separate budget allocations from the provost to support independent work by these academic units became consolidated. When students and faculty began working with residents and leaders of the Winstanley/Industry Park neighborhood they did so as part of interdisciplinary teams. They carried out this work under the direction of the faculty advisory committee comprised of professors from each of these units. As the project attracted faculty from other departments, such as: art, community psychology, dance, history, law, leisure studies, physics, and sociology representatives of these disciplines were added to the faculty advisory committee.

CREATING A ROBUST WEB PRESENCE: In 1991, Brian Orland, the only full professor participating in ESLARP, proposed spending approximately one-third of ESLARP's $100,000 budget to establish a worldwide web presence for the project. My initial response was quite negative. I felt the web was a tool that we simply could not afford, and I naively viewed it as little more than a "vanity" page for attention-seeking faculty. Demonstrating enormous patience, Brian described the multitude of ways in which we could use the web to advance our work. He explained how it would make our community partners and our own work significantly more visible to potential allies and external funders. He also described how we could share what he anticipated would be an enormous volume of valuable historical, environmental, economic, physical, political, and social data about East St. Louis among students, faculty, and third-party consultants working both simultaneously and sequentially on the project.

In addition, Brian articulated how the web could be used to maintain and analyze financial information for planning, management, and evaluation purposes. He speculated on how the web could be used to provide logistical support for the project by enabling us to post directions to the city, maps of the neighborhoods where students were working, lists of venders carrying frequently purchased project supplies, forms to track project expenses, and lists of local hotels/motels and restaurants available to house and feed volunteers. He also outlined how the web could be used to store technical memos on how to collect, organize, and analyze common forms of East St. Louis data. Finally, he explained how the web could host simple as well as complex computer models enabling student, faculty, and community members to undertake their own analysis of local conditions.

Over the years, the ESLARP website became one of our project's most valuable assets as hundreds of students and faculty participating in the project each semester used it to secure baseline data on the neighborhoods where they were working, download dozens of "field tested" survey instruments and interview schedules, preserve descriptive and analytical data on existing conditions, produce projections of future community conditions, and document the project's dizzying array of ongoing initiatives. Within two years of establishing the ESLARP website, it was receiving more external visits than the HUD's Community Outreach Partnership Center's website as students and faculty from campuses across the U.S. and overseas visited it to learn more about ESLARP's "bottom-up, bottom-sideways" approach planning and to access many of the training materials and research instruments developed by our faculty. One of the unexpected benefits resulting from ESLARP's web investment was the number of regional and national funders who ultimately supported several of our community partners after discovering them on our site.

Perhaps, the most impressive use of the web was as a platform for an integrated economic development model created by Professor Kieran Donaghy and later refined by Professor Varkki George Pallathucheril that allowed residents to compare and evaluate the environmental, economic, and social benefits and costs of alternative development projects using publicly available data. With only the dollar amount of a proposed investment and its industrial sector, ESLARP website users could determine the total number of jobs generated, income produced, and tax revenues created by competing projects. Using these same data, users could also estimate the costs of providing services for these new/expanded businesses, the land required to support these enterprises, and the dollars needed to mitigate the environmental impacts of these investments.

With these estimates ESLARP website users could generate cost-benefit ratios to identify the most economically and socially responsible and beneficial development projects. Equipped with a back-end report writing feature, the East St. Louis Urban Systems Model provided users with a straightforward explanation of these results. Pallathucheril and Orland subsequently integrated this environmental/economic model with an urban land use, zoning regulation, and urban design model that enabled users to evaluate the physical impact alternative developments might have on the built environment. Visitors to our website could tour proposed "redevelopment districts" to gain a deeper understanding of what that might look like and how they might function. Local stakeholders could also modify the basic assumptions of these models to produce their own independent analyses of competing development projects thereby improving the quality of local planning and design decision-making.

DEVELOPING A MULTI-PRONGED FUNDING STRATEGY: Rep. Younge's leadership role on the legislature's Higher Education Finance Committee guaranteed ESLARP the renewal of its annual state budget allocation of $100,000. This recurring source of funding, incorporated within the university budget, significantly enhanced the project's ability to secure complimentary public and private grants and contracts. ESLARP faculty sought additional recurring funding from a diverse set of sources. Two of ESLARP's most important sources of external funding were the City of East St. Louis and St. Clair County's CDBG programs, which matched the support ESLARP received from the state for many years. The second most important source of external support for ESLARP came from the HUD's Community Outreach Partnership Centers (COPC) program. This program, initiated by former HUD Secretary Henry G. Cisneros, provided up to $500,000 over a two-year period to universities willing to either initiate or significantly expand their work in severely distressed urban and rural communities.

ESLARP submitted an initial proposal that earmarked half of its proposed grant funds to our community partners in recognition of the value these groups brought to the partnership. HUD reviewers identified our commitment to sharing a significant portion of our grant funds as one of our proposal's most significant flaws. From HUD's perspective, this unusual budgetary arrangement was an acknowledgement by ESLARP that UIUC, acting alone, lacked the knowledge, skills, and competencies to launch and sustain an effective community/university development partnership. Following the rejection of our initial proposal, we entered into a spirited dialogue with the senior HUD staff regarding the contradiction between their partnership rhetoric and their privileging of universities over the community when it came to revenue-sharing. The following year, HUD changed its policies toward the kind of revenue sharing with community groups that we had initially proposed.

As a result, ESLARP received a two-year COPC Grant for $500,000 and a subsequent $100,000 institutionalization grant that enabled us to establish a fully staffed community organizing, planning, and development assistance office in the heart of East St. Louis. This one-stop community development assistance facility, called the East St. Louis Neighborhood Technical Assistance Center (NTAC) was staffed by a neighborhood organizer, community planner, architect/designer, and a grant writer. With the support of our COPC Grant, NTAC offered residents, business owners, religious leaders, non-profit executives, and local officials with promising community development ideas "cradle to grave" technical assistance to transform their ideas into reality.

One of NTAC's most important contributions to the city's recovery was its annual sponsorship, along with East St. Louis

Community Development Agency, East St. Louis Community Fund, and the Lessie Bates Davis Neighborhood House, of a five-day grantsmanship workshop conducted by San Francisco's Grantsmanship Center. The workshop enabled local stakeholders to conceptualize and refine a new community development project, prepare a compelling proposal for its development, and identify high-probability funders for this initiative. Each year this event enabled twelve to fifteen local organizations to develop community development grant applications that typically generated three to four times the amount of NTAC's budget to support the revitalization work being carried out by these groups. ESLARP's success in using its $100,000 in annual university funding to leverage significant amounts of third-party funds to advance its East St. Louis work led subsequent UIUC provosts and chancellors to raise the project's annual budget allocation to more than $200,000.

OFFERING OPPORTUNITIES TO EVALUATE ESLARP PROJECTS: ESLARP faculty began inviting local stakeholders to participate in an annual program retreat held in nearby Belleville, Illinois. Leaders from the neighborhoods and non-profit organizations with whom we were working, representatives of our major funders, ESLARP supported graduate research assistants and faculty participated in this annual two-day event. Grassroots leaders would meet in small groups, to discuss the progress they had achieved towards implementing their five-year development plans as well as the changes they would like to make during the next year to improve their effectiveness. Each neighborhood association and non-profit organization graded ESLARP's effectiveness in providing community organizing, issue research, comprehensive and strategic planning assistance, leadership development training and other technical assistance to their organizations using an A to D scale.

Representatives would offer their unvarnished evaluations of ESLARP. While ESLARP generally earned good marks, these evaluations always surfaced areas where our work had fallen short and needed to be improved. Embracing these public critiques in order to identify ways to improve our practice, communicated to our students the importance of learning from and with one's community partners. We typically invited each neighborhood association, non-profit organization, area funder, and municipal agency to identify the most important neighborhood and city-scale projects they believed ESLARP should undertake during the coming year. We would then work together to prioritize the projects to be completed during the coming year. In doing so, we shared ESLARP's detailed budget so local stakeholders would understand our resource limitations. Once the priorities were set by local leaders, ESLARP faculty would discuss with our East St. Louis partners how these projects could be most cost effectively carried out using university resources.

DEVELOPING ON CAMPUS RESOURCES: Over the years ESLARP made good use of the resources on campus to carry out our projects. This included the following

- Volunteers mobilized by UIUC student organizations were an ideal resource for one-day service projects such as neighborhood cleanups, small-scale landscape improvements and exterior home repairs.

- Students enrolled in large introductory courses requiring a service-learning component were an excellent resource for door knocking prior to community meetings, facilitation of small group exercises at larger neighborhood forums, and limited field-based data collection, entry, and analysis.

- Students participating in planning and design studios were a perfect resource for completing comprehensive district plans and designs or implementing medium to large-scale neighborhood improvement project, such as the Illinois Avenue Playground project.

- Individual theses students were a terrific resource for completing in-depth investigations of complex local issues, such as the East St. Louis' bond-for-deed housing market and its impact on neighborhood stability or the potential contribution crime prevention through environmental design practices might make towards improving public safety in East St. Louis' neighborhoods. Thesis students could also be extremely helpful in producing literature reviews, design concepts, architectural drawings, construction documents, preliminary budgets, and fundraising strategies for special housing facilities. A good example of such work was Kathryn Gregory's thesis on housing severely wounded and traumatized veterans that laid the foundation for the construction of the Eagles' Nest Veteran's Housing Complex in East St. Louis.

- Faculty buyouts for the design and completion of complex research and design projects were an ideal resource when the task at hand required a high level of specialized knowledge, considerable professional skill, and had to be completed in a timely manner. When East St. Louis began to experience a modest level of economic recovery in the late 1990s new investment became a possibility. These investments needed to be made in areas free of major environmental contaminants. Surveying and mapping existing environmental hazards using available local, state, and federal data and new data collected in the field required a high level or expertise. For this project, we brought out one of UIUC's health physicists who trained local high school students, their faculty, and area environmentalists to collect local samples and used UIUC's nuclear reactor to test the samples for more than two dozen forms of heavy metal contamination.

This faculty-led project provided local land use planners with critical information needed to safely site a wide range of community facilities. It also resulted in the publication of two frequently cited articles on soil sampling and heavy metal contamination in inner city neighborhoods published by a leading environmental science journal highlighting ESLARP's value as an important generator of research on environmental conditions in distressed urban communities. These ESLARP-funded buyouts, made possible through third-party grants, also allowed the project to expand the number of faculty and disciplines contributing to the project. Among the disciplines integrated into ESLARP during its early years through faculty buyouts were: anthropology, community psychology, history, law, leisure studies, physics, and sociology.

On those rare occasions when local residents were committed to action projects that exceeded ESLARP's available resources, residents and funders, committed to these initiatives would often work together to find the additional funds to complete these projects. ESLARP's highly transparent and participatory approach to program planning, management, and evaluation relieved faculty from being solely responsible for project selection. Participating community residents, institutional leaders, municipal officials, area funders and UIUC faculty and students were now cooperatively making these decisions reducing the likelihood of UIUC faculty and administrators being criticized by local groups for selecting projects that advanced their interests at the community's expense.

INCENTIVE-BASED RECRUITMENT: If a department committed itself to participating in ESLARP's "work weekends," we offered to cover their travel, lodging, and other fieldwork-related expenses. If a department incorporated an East St. Louis service-learning component into one of their large intro courses, the project offered to support the costs of a graduate assistant and fieldwork expenses for these classes. If a department offered a workshop/studio focused on East St. Louis we subsidized the costs of a graduate assistant and fieldwork-related expenses. During a challenging fiscal period for public universities, these incentives prompted a number of departments to become regularly involved in resident-led research, planning, design, and development projects in East St. Louis. These material incentives for departmental involvement in ESLARP were complimented by a variety of administrative, logistical, and technological services that made East St. Louis fieldwork a bit easier than in other communities. For example, a wide range of East St. Louis-related census data and maps were already available for use by UIUC faculty on ESLARP's website. In addition, ESLARP faculty was available for in-depth orientations to East St. Louis classes as they began their work in the city.

EMBRACING TENURE-SENSITIVE POLICIES: At the time ESLARP was launched, junior faculty in most UIUC departments, were discouraged from participating in labor-intensive, community-based research projects by senior faculty concerned about the impact such activities might have on their tenure and promotion prospects. Sensitive to these concerns, ESLARP faculty sought ways to reward the contributions junior faculty made to the project. The founding ESLARP faculty made a strong commitment to disseminating the results of our community-based research, planning, and design efforts in East St. Louis through scholarly publications. In doing so, we adopted a policy of listing, as co-authors, the faculty who made significant contributions to the work being described and listed the tenure-track faculty first so as to privilege their contributions in the eyes of those sitting on departmental, college, and university promotion and tenure committees at UIUC.

When pursuing third-party funding for our East St. Louis work, we listed all contributing ESLARP faculty as co-principal investigators on the project. Whenever possible we listed the tenure-track faculty as the PIs on these projects. This policy further enhanced the profile of ESLARP's junior faculty who were centrally involved in these efforts as they approached tenure. As the project began to receive national attention resulting in invitations to give lectures on campuses throughout the United States and keynote presentations at a variety of higher education conferences, we recommended our non-tenured faculty for these roles to further strengthen their CVs as they began moving through what was becoming an increasingly competitive promotion and tenure process.

PROMOTING ESLARP AT NATIONAL CONFERENCES: In his classic volume *On War,* Carl Von Clausewitz discussed the value of the "indirect approach" to modern warfare. One of the most effective ways ESLARP faculty discovered to bring positive recognition to our East St. Louis work was to host national conferences that brought the project's "bottom-up, bottom-sideways" planning and design efforts to the attention of leading citizens, professionals, scholars, journalists, philanthropists, and policy-makers throughout the U.S. and abroad. In May 1995, ESLARP hosted the Annual Conference of Planners' Network, a national organization comprised of progressive planning and design students, practicing architects and planners, grassroots activists, urban scholars, and elected officials, that brought more than 600 visitors to the city. The selection of East St. Louis as the conference site, over Philadelphia, Boston, and Amherst, generated a great deal of local excitement and press attention. This was, according

Dr. David Westendorff, Senior Policy Analyst for the (UNRISD), addresses the opening session of the Planners' Network in East St. Louis (Photo by ESLARP Staff).

the East St. Louis Mayor's Office, the first significant conference to be held in the city since 1974. The local host committee, comprised of East St. Louis residents, nonprofit managers, city officials, and ESLARP faculty, decided to structure the event as a "working conference" to tap the knowledge and skills of the event's participants. It made this a transformative experience for the attendees.

Neighborhood leaders took conference participants to communities whose residents were seeking assistance in addressing thorny local planning issues.

Following resident-led tours, participants were presented with the details of a messy planning/design problem confronting residents. Provided with detailed information regarding this issue, conference participants were given four hours to consider alternative solutions, select a recommended course of action, and identify immediate, short, and long-term implementation steps. The results were then briefly presented at a dinnertime assembly held at city hall. The conference's "community charettes" generated dozens of innovative solutions to several of the city's most pressing problems.

Lamar Gentry, East St Louis City Manager, presenting ESLARP Day Proclamation to Prof. Reardon and Dan Hoffman, Executive Director of ESLARP prior to the beginning of the Planners' Network Conference, 1995

A dozen or more of these proposals were implemented, in the years following the conference, by local community-based organizations with ESLARP's assistance.

In 1997, ESLARP hosted the annual conference of the HUD's Community Outreach Partnership Center that involved more than 300 grassroots leaders, municipal planners, and university scholars from cities funded under this program. Following a format similar to the 1995 Planners' Network Conference, this event involved a broader range of East St. Louis stakeholders who worked with conference participants to address a second, and in many ways, more ambitious set of local issues. The selection of East St. Louis as a conference site, by two national organizations, based not on the severity of its problems but the innovative manner in which local stakeholders and university scholars were using participatory means to address these issues challenged the "necropolis" image of East St. Louis held by many residents, officials, and journalists from the greater St. Louis metropolitan region.

PARTICIPATING IN THE UNITED NATIONS' VOLUNTARY ACTION FOR LOCAL DEMOCRACY PROJECT: While organizing the 1995 Planners' Network Conference, I reached out to one of my former Cornell University classmates, David Westendorff, to ask if he and his colleagues at the UN's Research Institute in Social Development (NRISD) might be interested in participating in the event. David gave the conference's initial plenary lecture placing the city's environmental, economic, and social problems within the context of a rapidly globalizing economy and increasingly influential neo-conservative urban policies. In addition, David's agency agreed to fund the participation of a dozen grassroots activists from the Chiapas Province of Mexico, the northern cone of Lima, Peru, and central Bangkok, Thailand.

ESLARP subsequently received a formal invitation to join UNRISD's Voluntary Action for Local Democracy Project, giving us the opportunity to present our work at the international social forums sponsored by the UN prior to the Social Summit in Copenhagen and the HABITAT II Summit in Istanbul. Participation in these UN-sponsored events, in turn, led to ESLARP being invited by the newly-elected Workers' Party government of Brazil to participate in an urban transformation conference held in Porto Alegre and a community-planning forum hosted at the University of San Paulo. Scholarly publications related to these international forums, as well as local press coverage, highlighting our participation in these "invitation only" international forums, significantly enhanced ESLARP's standing in the region, the University of Illinois system, and urban and regional planning scholarly community.

Through these international conferences and related publications, ESLARP became recognized as a well-known example of resident-led urban transformation in South America, Europe, Africa, and

Prof. Reardon (far right) participates in NGO Forum at the UN Social Development Summit in Copenhagen (Photo courtesy of UNRISD Staff).

Asia. In recent years, former ESLARP faculty been invited to share lessons learned regarding equity planning and participatory policy-making at McGill University, University of Toronto, and University of Manitoba in Canada; Sheffield University in the UK; National Technical University in Norway; Rome IV University, Sapienza University and the University of Catania in Italy; Technion University in Israel; Tongje University in Shanghai, China, and Maynooth University in Ireland. In addition, ESLARP has been described as a leading example of effective equity planning, participatory design and transformative education by leading urban theorists including: John Forester, Leonie Sandercock, Tom Angotti, Scott Peters, and Anne Khadamian.

12. LIGHT RAIL AND HOUSING PROJECTS IN EAST ST. LOUIS

ESLARP'S INCREASED ORGANIZATIONAL capacity allowed it to expand its neighborhood planning activities in the mid-to-late 1990s into East St. Louis' Edgemont, Alta Sita, and South End neighborhoods. In 1996 and 1997, ESLARP students prepared comprehensive plans for these areas while undertaking a growing list of small and medium-scale improvement projects in neighborhoods where we had previously worked. These efforts were made possible by the additional staff funded through ESLARP's Community Outreach Partnership Center grant. This HUD funding not only assisted ESLARP in establishing its East St. Louis Neighborhood Technical Assistance Center but it also enabled the project to hire its first full-time project coordinator to manage its growing number of grant-funded graduate research assistants, and coordinate its increasingly popular volunteer "work weekends." These programs often engaged more than eighty students and faculty working on a half dozen unique outreach, field research, cleanup, and construction projects during a single weekend.

In the fall of 1997, I received an early morning call from Ceola Davis who excitedly informed me that the Bi-State Development Agency responsible for transportation planning within the greater St. Louis metropolitan region was considering a plan to construct a light rail line connecting St. Louis International Airport with the city's central business district. Upon hearing the proposal, Davis immediately saw the economic development potential of the light rail line for East St. Louis residents and business persons provided the planners and policy-makers could be convinced to extend the proposed light rail line eastward over the Mississippi River through East St. Louis' poorest neighborhoods.

With the assistance of ESLARP's first project coordinator, Dan Hoffman, who had significant urban transportation experience as a former planner and policy analyst in Trenton, New Jersey and

Philadelphia, Pennsylvania, the faculty advisory committee recruited professors from UIUC's anthropology, architecture, economics, landscape architecture, and urban planning programs to conduct a feasibility study evaluating the potential benefits of an extended light rail line serving the entire metro east region not simply the St. Louis, Missouri portion of the region.

While students and faculty from these departments evaluated the environmental, economic, social benefits, and costs of an extended line and explored alternative routes aimed at serving the greatest number of transit-dependent East St. Louisans, allies of the Emerson Park Development Corporation quietly began purchasing parcels adjacent to the most likely site for an Emerson Park station along the proposed light rail line extension. This land assembly effort, which we referred to as "speculation for social justice," was pursued with ESLARP's assistance to provide these local organizations with needed leverage when negotiating with developers who might be attracted to the areas surrounding proposed station sites on the Illinois side of the river. The most likely Emerson Park station stop boasted fabulous views of the historic old St. Louis Courthouse, the Gateway Arch and provided extremely short commutes to St. Louis's central business district and Lambert Field's industrial and warehouse districts. In addition, much of the land surrounding the likely Emerson Park station was publicly owned making it easy to assemble parcels for a major development.

As our students worked on the feasibility report and routing study, an unmarked envelope appeared at the NTAC. This package contained records showing a number of close friends and allies of several powerful local officials purchasing land along the Route 64 right-of-way in East St. Louis that many believed, despite its obvious shortcomings, to be the most likely East St. Louis route, for an extended St. Louis Metro Link System. While we never learned who provided these documents to us, they certainly increased the leverage grassroots leaders had when encouraging municipal officials to consider our alternative route that provided mobility to the maximum number of transit-dependent, low-income, East St. Louis families.

In mid-December 1997, more than 100 neighborhood residents, institutional leaders, and elected officials from East St. Louis gathered in the gymnasium of the Lessie Bates Davis Neighborhood House to hear a presentation of our students' feasibility report and routing study. Attending the meeting as invited guests were Mayor Bush and the chairperson of the Bi-State Development Agency, both of whom had already voiced strong support for the original, Missouri-only, St. Louis Metro Link System proposal as members of the Metropolitan Planning Organization (MPO). Ceola Davis and her EPDC colleagues, working with what had become a strong network of community-based development organizations affiliated with ESLARP, did an impressive job mobilizing local stakeholders to attend this meeting. Davis and her neighbors also supervised the set-up of the room that placed the East St. Louis Mayor and his MPO colleague at the center of the gymnasium surrounded by residents. The chairs reserved for these officials were uncomfortable, unstable and extremely well lit by overhead lights. Davis explained, "These men are seasoned politicians with extensive experience dealing with community groups, so the room with its uncomfortable chairs and extreme lighting represent our effort to level the playing field a bit!"

Our students presented a brief history and status report on the MPO's St. Louis Metro Link Light Rail proposal then summarized the major findings of their feasibility report evaluating a possible extension of the proposed light rail line eastward over the Mississippi River through East St. Louis terminating at Scott Air Force Base in Belleville, Illinois. Among the major points our students made were the following:

- The vast majority of light rail systems built in the United States experience significant operating deficits due to high fixed costs, low population densities, and modest ridership by consumers having considerable choice regarding modes of transportation.

- A light rail line designed to bring business and tourist travelers to and from St. Louis' CBD and St Louis International Airport is likely to operate at a significant annual deficit that will, over time, require increasing public subsidies.

- Operating deficits for the proposed St. Louis Metro Link System, initially limited to the St. Louis County portion of the region, could be dramatically reduced by extending the system eastward to serve East St. Louis and other nearby St. Clair County communities. While the population densities of East St. Louis and its surrounding collar towns are modest, the percentage of transit-dependent families in these communities is quite high, thereby, significantly increasing overall system ridership. There would also be a considerable number of suburban St. Clair County riders seeking to avoid the increasing congestion on the region's east/west river crossings as well as the increasing costs of long daily commutes given rising gasoline prices.

- While most light rail systems feature significant ridership into the CBD from suburban locations in the mornings and similarly high ridership from the CBD to the suburbs in the afternoons and evenings, the extension of the system eastward into and through East St. Louis would provide the system with a significant population of reverse commuters comprised of local residents riding the system to soon-to-be-accessible living wage jobs in St. Louis' CBD and near St. Louis' Lambert Field.

- The proposed system serving the Missouri side of the river would improve access to regional educational, health, employment, and cultural facilities for residents who are already quite mobile and have considerable choice of transportation modes while offering nothing to the region's poorest and most transportation "underserved" residents whose tax dollars would be used, in part, to fund these improvements thereby undermining transportation equity within the region—in possible violation of The Civil Rights Act of 1964.

- A light rail system, such as the one initially proposed by the leadership of the Bi-State Development Agency, would face considerable political opposition from elected officials representing the Illinois whose residents would not benefit from this light rail investment.

The students concluded that an extension of the light rail system from the St. Louis waterfront to Scott Air Force Base made excellent environmental, economic, and social sense. The enthusiastic response this recommendation received prompted Mayor Bush to rise and say, "I am in full agreement with the results of the UIUC report. I am prepared to ask the city council to endorse the proposed extension of the system. Do you also have a recommended route for your proposed East St. Louis extension?"

At that point, Davis asked two youngsters standing next to a large piece of blank paper hanging on the gymnasium wall to pull the cords they were holding revealing the proposed route that EPDC and its sister neighborhood organizations had devised with considerable assistance from UIUC planners and designers. The proposed route required the least number of public "takings" of private properties, and served the largest number of metro east families without cars, providing these families with life changing access to living wage employment in downtown St. Louis and near the airport. Davis asked Mayor Bush to endorse what she referred to as the "Laser Line Extension," and he agreed.

Honoring his commitment, Mayor Bush subsequently convinced the East St. Louis City Council to withdraw their earlier support for Bi-State's "Missouri-only" light rail plan in favor of EPDC's new "Two State" light rail solution. Several weeks after the East St. Louis City Council withdrew its support for Bi-State's initial plan, the agency voted in favor of the community-generated "Two State" proposal. Having secured Bi-State Development Corporation's support for their rail line proposal, Davis and her colleagues asked influential Illinois U.S. Senators Paul Simon and Dick Durban for their assistance in persuading federal transportation officials to fund the newly extended system. With their help the additional funds needed to construct the extended system were appropriated.

Davis asked the ESLARP faculty advisory committee to work with EPDC to update the community's six-year-old Emerson Park Neighborhood Improvement Plan making the following arguments:

- EPDC had successfully completed the overwhelming majority of the neighborhood stabilization projects contained in its original plan.

- These improvements, along with the federal government's decision to fund the East St. Louis segment of the St. Louis Metro Link System, necessitated a shift from stabilization to revitalization policies, programs, and projects.

- A failure to expand quality-housing options for local residents who would soon have access to living wage jobs in downtown St. Louis and near Lambert Field, could lead to significant outmigration of working families from Emerson Park undermining the neighborhood's stability.

"If we don't provide families who will soon have members of their households taking the Metro Link to well-paying jobs across the river with quality affordable housing, they will be tempted, as their incomes, savings, and credit scores improve, to move elsewhere," she argued.

We recruited a new Ph.D. student in Urban and Regional Planning, Janni Sorensen, to organize a new neighborhood planning workshop whose students would prepare a growth-oriented plan for Emerson Park featuring a significant amount of new workforce housing. While the Emerson Park Neighborhood Improvement Plan of 1991 had concentrated on environmental mitigation, crime prevention, and emergency home repairs to stem the flow of investment, businesses, and residents from the area; the Emerson Park Revitalization Plan of 1997 would focus on infrastructure, education, and housing investments designed to help "grow" the neighborhood.

EPDC leaders and ESLARP faculty believed the community development organization was poised to undertake a significant redevelopment project that could transform the area. However, the community and campus leaders most deeply involved in the creation of the new Emerson Park plan believed they needed an experienced real estate developer with a strong commitment to participatory planning, to partner with them on the plan's affordable housing element.

Faculty, EPDC leadership and residents speculated about the possibility of recruiting the St. Louis-based, McCormack Baron Company, as their partner for the "new town/in town" development featured in the Emerson Park Revitalization Plan of 1997. Richard Baron had begun his career as a Legal Services attorney who frequently sued the St. Louis Housing Authority on behalf of public housing tenants as well as suburban St. Louis "collar towns" that practiced exclusionary zoning to prevent the construction of multi-family housing within their jurisdictions. Residents were impressed by Baron's development philosophy that emphasized the importance of addressing the environmental, economic, and social aspects of community development in a holistic manner, especially through the development of strong public schools, living wage jobs, and accessible health care. Finally, they were impressed by the design and construction quality of McCormack Baron's St. Louis housing complexes as well as the company's hands-on approach to property management. Unfortunately, no one involved in ESLARP had a relationship with Baron or any of the principals in his firm.

Before we could identify someone from our network that could introduce us to Baron, Prof. Andrejasich and I received an invitation to make a presentation to a group of area real estate executives that included Baron. We provided a snapshot of recent developments taking place in East St. Louis and its surrounding suburban collar towns. After describing the grassroots movement that had brought UIUC students and faculty to East St. Louis, we discussed the community's need to identify a visionary developer to partner with the city's expanding network of CDCs on larger scale projects.

We told the story of EPDC's slow progression from cleaning-up properties, constructing small-scale playgrounds, scraping and painting the homes of low-income individuals to constructing, with Habitat for Humanity, a limited number of in-fill units. We then described EPDC's latest proposal to construct a "new town/in town" community affordable to poor and working-class families. We wrapped-up our presentation paraphrasing the recruitment motto of the U.S. Marine Corp, "The United States Marines - Looking for a Few Good Men! The Emerson Park Development Corporation—Looking for a Developer with Prophetic Vision and Intestinal Fortitude!"

While our presentation generated a few chuckles and a modest amount of polite applause, we were exclusively focused on whether or not we had impressed Baron. He stopped us on our way out of the meeting room, handed us his business card, and invited us to call him to arrange a meeting. Within a few weeks of this encounter, key ESLARP faculty and graduate research assistants working on the implementation of the Emerson Park Revitalization Plan were sitting in Baron's St. Louis headquarters with members of his senior staff.

Baron reviewed, in considerable detail, what he liked about our recently completed Emerson Park plan and complemented the community vision, overall development goal, specific improvement objectives, and proposed action strategies. However, he felt the affordable housing proposals were insufficiently ambitious and unlikely to be funded in their current form. He described how his company, working with EPDC, could generate forty percent more new housing units than we had programmed through a mix of HOPE VI, Low Income Tax Credit, and conventional mortgage financing.

His staff then described a proposed location, architectural style, unit costs, public amenities, property management, and monthly costs for renters and homeowners for a new 140-unit mixed-income development. In doing so, they explained how their proposal reflected our stakeholders' key housing preferences as summarized in our plan. Baron then described the challenges of urban real estate that made it an unsuitable activity for the "faint of heart." After stating his strong desire to work with EPDC in the implementation of our housing strategy, he said the organization and its leaders needed to be sure they were ready to make the shift from grassroots activists to co-developers of a major affordable housing project. Before entering into a development partnership with McCormack Baron, he suggested a series of Sunday evening seminars on the thrills, spills, and chills of contemporary urban real estate development for EPDC's core leaders and supporters. If EPDC was still interested in getting involved in the urban real estate game following this series he said he would then like to show them a few of his St. Louis projects that reflected many of the concepts and strategies that he felt would work well in East St. Louis.

Over the course of the next four weeks, a group of fifteen Emerson Park leaders and ESLARP students and faculty participated in Urban Real Estate 101 conducted by Baron's staff. At the end of this series, a vanload of EPDC leaders spent a day touring several McCormack Baron housing complexes in St. Louis. Impressed by the firm's desire to ensure that EPDC was ready to undertake a major housing development project and pleased by the quality of the McCormack Baron projects they visited, EPDC decided to enter into a partnership with Richard Baron to produce 140 units of mixed-income, mixed-financed housing in Emerson Park.

Over the course of the next year, McCormack Baron staff worked closely with EPDC leaders, local institutions, municipal officials, and ESLARP faculty and staff to produce site plans, architectural and construction drawings, and budgets for the construction of a mixed-income, mixed-finance development called Parsons Place. It featured 140 units of Craftsman-inspired rental and homeowner housing units, a Caribbean-inspired central park, a Montessori-based pre-school, and a community center. Between 1998 and 2000, construction was completed and Parsons Place was fully occupied, attracting a mix of teachers, police officers, fire fighters, social service and health care professionals, casino workers, hospitality industry employees, and retirees. It was a quality housing development serving the local community's needs that EPDC activists, and their ESLARP colleagues, would never have imagined in 1990.

13. THE EAST ST. LOUIS NEIGHBORHOOD COLLEGE

IN THE SPRING OF 1997, my ESLARP colleagues and I found ourselves faced with criticisms from our closest and most highly regarded community partners. We drove to what we thought was a routine EPDC meeting at the Neighborhood House, however, as my graduate assistants and I pulled into the parking lot we noticed a number of vehicles belonging to community leaders from other parts of the city. I realized we were about to be special guests at an accountability session.

Looking around the room I saw local leaders holding copies of one of the first articles I published on ESLARP's empowerment approach to community planning. As usual, Ceola Davis chaired the meeting to which representatives from the various neighborhoods where ESLARP was active, including Emerson Park, Lansdowne, Winstanley/Industry Park, Olivette Park, Edgemont, Alta Sita, and South End were present.

She described the positive opinion those assembled had of ESLARP's local community planning and development efforts. In fact, she stated that everyone gathered at the Neighborhood House that afternoon believed their relationship with ESLARP was one of the most respectful and beneficial partnerships with an outside institution they had ever had. She then went on to explain how their respect for the UIUC students and faculty with whom they were working had prompted today's meeting focused on the nature of our relationship. Referring to my article, Davis asked if we were still committed to the empowerment approach to planning outlined in my paper? Without hesitation, I said, "Absolutely!" Davis responded by saying, "Great, so are we! However, we want to discuss the substantial gulf that exists between the language contained in your article and ESLARP's day-to-day practices."

EPDC's Richard Suttle explained, "UIUC recruits many of the most talented students from Illinois and the nation. Still, you find it necessary to provide the students participating in ESLARP with 9 to 15 credits of community planning, urban design, non-profit management, and business communication education each semester to prepare them for their East St. Louis work. On the other hand, most of us have never had an opportunity to spend a single day studying at a university like UIUC, yet ESLARP hasn't provided neighborhood leaders with a single class to prepare us for our role in this important partnership. Such practices reduce our role to that of the flea on the tail of the dog." The lack of secondary and higher education and previous leadership experience among residents working on policy-making boards created by ESLARP frequently left them feeling like "participants" without real voice or influence.

"Offering those excluded from power for generations seats at the table is not enough to insure them influence over the process," explained Davis. "We know you did not intend to do it, but you have created a project that has reproduced a racist approach to community development that privileges the needs, opinions, and ideas of university-trained professionals over those of local leaders," she said.

The concrete proposal local leaders made for remedying this situation was the establishment of Highlander-like center for the training and development of local leaders, similar to the one established in Tennessee in the 1930s where many of the nation's civil rights leaders were trained. With this training, community activists and leaders could move from being observers and minor contributors to ESLARP's collaborative planning and development efforts to being actual co-designers and co-managers of these efforts.

Among the specific courses local leaders said they were most eager to see the East St. Louis Neighborhood College offer were:

- Fundamentals of Direct Action Organizing

- Principles of Participatory Planning and Design

- Introduction to Non-Profit Organization and Management

- The ABC's of Conflict Resolution

- Community-Based Crime Prevention

- Affordable Housing Production and Management
- Managerial and Financial Accounting
- Grantsmanship 101
- Program Monitoring and Evaluation

Local leaders believed these courses would have their greatest impact if they were co-taught by long-time community leaders and ESLARP faculty members. During the ride back to campus, my colleagues and I shared our considerable surprise, disappointment, and rage over what we described as our "woodshed" meeting. I sustained a lengthy, profanity-laced, harangue highlighting the intellectual, moral, political, and psycho-sexual shortcomings of our long-term partners who, from my perspective, did not appreciate the risks we were taking as untenured professors to pursue engaged scholarship in East St. Louis. Pulling off I-55/70 in Effingham, Illinois for gas, I looked at my colleagues who had endured my long harangue of the residents' critique of our model, burst into laughter and said, "How could we have been so stupid? They are absolutely right! By providing our students with increasing levels of community planning and development training while not offering similar learning opportunities to our community partners we were absolutely making an already uneven playing field more challenging!" When I asked rhetorically, "How could we have failed to see this problem?" One of my colleagues responded with one of Ceola Davis' favorite quotes, "The fish are always the last to know they live in water."

Returning to campus, we convened a meeting of the faculty advisory committee to share our community partners' critique of our project model. Like me, the faculty was both shocked and angered by the residents' characterization of our work as neo-colonial. Advisory committee members cited our longstanding practice of having residents select the projects to be worked on, participate in determining the research designs to be followed, shape the surveys and interview schedules to be used, and collaborate in the data analysis and plan-making phases of the process. One advisory committee member asked, "What other university research project offers community residents as many meaningful opportunities to shape the work being done as ours?" I responded by saying, "They are not criticizing us for failing to involve them in the process; they are criticizing us for not offering them the kind of training that we felt our own students needed to be effective in a challenging setting such as East St. Louis." Once the faculty got over the initial damage to our egos, we began to view the criticisms as evidence of the degree to which the city's grassroots leaders had come to embrace ESLARP's strong commitment to reciprocal learning, participatory planning, and democratic design.

After considerable discussion, advisory committee members embraced our community partners' proposal to establish the East St. Louis Neighborhood College. We also discussed how we, as a group of faculty strongly committed to social justice, could have structured ESLARP so that it significantly limited the role of those Antonio Gramsci referred to as "organic intellectuals" from the community. Some attributed this error to our preoccupation with preparing the next generation of inspired architects, landscape architects, and urban planners. Others argued that our knowledge of the often-insensitive work carried out by earlier generations of UIUC researchers in East St. Louis had caused us to focus too much attention on the role of students in the partnership. Several faculty members attributed our near-exclusive concern with student development to our need as "subject-matter experts" to maintain control over the teaching/planning process. One faculty member attributed our inability to critically examine our East St. Louis work to the embarrassing number of awards for research and practice excellence that we had individually and collectively received. While pleased to receive such recognition, we often felt that we were being honored by members of the planning and design communities because we were working with a segment of our society (namely extremely low-income African-Americans) that many of our academic and professional colleagues were simply not prepared to work with.

We began to work with neighborhood leaders to organize the first course they requested: an eight-week class on direct action organizing. After speaking with Davis, I agreed to co-teach an eight-week course on the origins, evolution, and current state of grassroots organizing with her. This inaugural course of the East St. Louis Neighborhood College was scheduled to take place at Southern Illinois University's East St. Louis Center on eight consecutive Saturdays during the spring of 1997.

While appreciative of the community's strong desire to access relevant community organizing, planning, design, development, and management classes through ESLARP, the faculty was also aware of the many responsibilities that East St. Louis' mostly female, grassroots leaders had to juggle on Saturdays. While I prepared twenty-five packets containing the course syllabus and readings, I wasn't sure the class would attract more than a handful of residents on Saturdays. This was the day when the majority of East St. Louisans, most of whom who did not have access to private cars, used the city's shaky bus system to do their weekly grocery shopping, take their families' clothing to the laundry, and bring their children to the barber shop and beauty salon for hair day. I was delighted when upon entering the classroom I saw Ceola Davis, my co-instructor, standing in front of forty-three adults.

During the next eight weeks I was thrilled to see so many of the key neighborhood leaders with whom we were working as well as several human service professionals, the First Assistant U.S. Attorney, and a local bank president who had financed several of our housing rehabilitation projects participate in the class. During the class we explored:

- Power and Its Importance
- The Origins and Evolution of Direct Action Organizing in the US
- The Key Principles of Direct Action Organizing
- Identifying and Defining "Actionable/Winnable" Issues
- Designing a Direct Action Organizing Campaign
- Crafting Winning Organizing Strategies and Tactics
- Recruiting Members and Developing Leaders
- Preparing Leaders for Action

Prof. Reardon co-teaching with Miss Ceola Davis the East St. Louis
Neighborhood College's first class on community organizing
(Photo by ESLARP Staff).

As the class approached its seventh week several students asked
if we could extend the course by three additional weeks to cover several important topics that we had mentioned but not fully explored.
While I have occasionally had a class during my thirty-year career in
higher education run a bit longer than the scheduled course time. I
have never experienced the kind of unbridled student interest, curi-
osity, and passion for learning these East St. Louis residents displayed
that prompted them to stay late each week and request a three-week
extension of the class.

Early in the course, two young African-American men wearing
suits appeared in the class. I invited these young men to tell us their
names, identify what group they were affiliated with, and share
their reasons for attending the class. When they appeared reluctant,
I reminded them they were among friends and didn't need to be
nervous. At that point, one of the young men said he was not sure we
would feel that way when he told us why he and his associate were
there. He then went on to explain that the mayor's chief of staff had
asked them to find out what was taking place during what many city
hall insiders were calling the "Saturday Morning Bolshevik Brunch
Club." Suttle, sensing their discomfort, welcomed them to the class
and hoping to make them feel more comfortable asked, "What did

you do down at city hall that got you assigned to Saturday morning 'detention' with us?" As the class laughed, Suttle reached over, shook the two young men's hands, and welcomed them to the club.

During the next two years, more than one hundred and fifty hundred East St. Louis leaders participated in nearly a dozen Neighborhood College classes, co-taught by neighborhood leaders and UIUC faculty. One of the most significant outcomes of these classes was the formation in 1998 of a citywide association of citizen organizations committed to enhancing the political voice of poor and working-class East St. Louisans in municipal planning, design, and development decision-making. For several years in the late 1990s and early 2000s, the East St. Louis Community Action Network (ESLCAN) carried out a series of direct-action organizing campaigns using principles and techniques we had studied in our first class to promote more equitable redevelopment policies and participatory decision-making processes within the city. This coalition, which was strictly non-partisan, did, however, quietly support several reform candidates for City Council who succeeded in handing the East St. Louis and St. Clair County Democratic Organizations their first electoral defeats in more than fifty years.

When ESLARP organized an extended annual program review in 1998, on the tenth anniversary of the university's East St. Louis initiative, residents cited the establishment of the East St. Louis Neighborhood College as one of the project's most important accomplishments. Quoting one of the original students from our community organizing class, who like many others carried their battered course reader around as an important reference book, "As an older African-American woman from Mississippi I never imagined going to college. However, I hoped someday that my daughter or granddaughter would have the opportunity to attend college. Sadly, neither of them has been able to do so. So, you can imagine what it meant to me to finally attend college classes through this program."

14. A DECADE OF LESSONS LEARNED

WORKING WITH CEOLA DAVIS and her East St. Louis neighbors for nearly ten years taught my students and I many important lessons. Among the most of these were:

TREND IS NOT DESTINY!

The accomplishments of ESLARP and its community partners between 1990 and 2000 offer compelling evidence of Rene Dubois' famous statement, "Whenever human beings are concerned, trend is not destiny." At the beginning of the project, very few community leaders, municipal officials, area funders, regional policy-makers, or university scholars believed much could be done to revitalize older residential neighborhoods in failing industrial centers such as East St. Louis. However, a small group of determined Emerson Park women inspired by the civil rights-era work of Fannie Lou Hamer and Ella Baker and the more recent community transformation efforts of Rep. Younge and Katherine Dunham believed otherwise.

The partnership formed between the women, who established the Emerson Park Development Corporation, and the UIUC students and faculty, who organized the East St. Louis Action Research Project, laid the foundation for a highly productive collaboration that prospered for more than twenty-five years. Stakeholders from the city's Emerson Park, Lansdowne, Winstanley/Industry Park, Olivette Park, Edgemont, Alta Sita and South End neighborhoods implemented dozens of small and medium-scale improvement projects that stabilized, and in the case of Emerson Park, substantially revitalized their communities. In the process of doing so, these residents helped seed a municipal reform movement that elected several community-minded city councilpersons who fought for more progressive and responsible governance in East St. Louis.

BUILD A POPULAR BASE FOR MUNICIPAL REFORM

The economic and community development projects undertaken by this partnership were made possible through the collective efforts of neighborhood associations, community development corporations, a city-wide citizen action organization, and a community development assistance center that ESLARP students and faculty played a pivotal role in either establishing or strengthening. The failure of ESLARP's early efforts to support Emerson Park residents' efforts to implement key elements of their plan forced faculty to acknowledge the limitations of their original participatory action research approach to community planning in East St. Louis. While participatory action research methods enabled ESLARP to engage local residents in co-producing a plan that a broad cross-section of the community supported, these methods did not help them assemble these interests into a politically effective organization capable of overcoming the control the East St. Louis and St. Clair County Democratic Organizations exerted over local government policy-making.

Recognizing the corrosive effect that long-term suburbanization, disinvestment, and outmigration had on the number, size, and effectiveness of citizen organizations representing East St. Louis' poor and working-class families, ESLARP faculty integrated a robust organizing element into their community planning to overcome the extreme concentration of political power that existed within the city. Beginning in 1991, ESLARP struggled to incorporate key elements of direct action organizing into their participatory action research-based approach to comprehensive planning. Before initiating comprehensive planning efforts in other neighborhoods, ESLARP faculty challenged local leaders to form steering committees representing existing community-based organizations to provide leadership to these efforts. ESLARP faculty also trained community residents and university students engaged in local surveying, interviewing, and focus groups in these areas to view these interactions with local stakeholders as both data collection efforts and grassroots organizing opportunities. In addition, they encouraged East St. Louis field researchers to end every interaction with local stakeholders with a personal invitation to become actively involved in the organizing process underway in their neighborhood.

ESLARP faculty was influenced by Saul Alinsky's commitment to grassroots leadership development. Therefore, throughout the planning process being co-facilitated by community-based organizations and ESLARP, leaders and staff consistently challenged themselves to identify and develop neighborhood residents whose organizing, communication, and management skills could be further developed through their successful performance of a series of increasingly demanding leadership roles required by ESLARP's highly participatory planning approach. While ESLARP faculty expected students to carry out the majority of the outreach, agenda development, meeting set-up, group facilitation and reporting, and meeting evaluation responsibilities during the early part of local planning processes, students were expected to recruit, prepare, and support resident leaders to assume these roles as these processes evolved.

Using this process to establish and strengthen community-based organizations in the city's poor and working-class communities that had, according to Robert Putnam in *Bowling Alone,* been savagely undermined by powerful global forces in the 1970s and 1980s, ESLARP students and faculty viewed the community-organizing/building aspect of the project to be as important as the plan-making and urban design aspects of the project. If the planning and design process being used did not contribute to expanding the popular base for municipal reform in East St. Louis, ESLARP faculty believed there would be little opportunity for the plans to be implemented within the city's "machine-controlled" political environment.

EMBRACE RECIPROCITY

UIUC had a presence in East St. Louis, in the form of its Cooperative Extension Service and the Urban Extension and Minority Access Project, for decades prior to ESLARP's establishment in 1991. During this time, most local residents were unaware of the economic and community developments programs being carried out by these university units. Among the small number of East St. Louis residents familiar with UIUC's community development assistance efforts, few viewed these programs as central to the city's recovery. Most resident leaders believed the majority of UIUC's programs were short-term initiatives designed to generate data needed to support the publishing efforts of faculty seeking promotion and tenure. While UIUC's extension staff and research faculty spent hundreds of thousands of dollars in East St. Louis and St. Clair County each year, few of these expenditures, with the exception of Head Start and the Expanded Food and Nutrition Education Programs (EFNEP), appeared to touch the lives of those living in the city's poorest neighborhoods.

Overcoming the cynical view residents of the city's poorest neighborhoods had of the university's past efforts required a radical change in approach and Davis provided the impetus for this change. The principles for non-exploitive community/university collaboration contained in the Ceola Accords prompted ESLARP to abandon traditional approaches to urban research that privileged the needs of the campus over the community, in favor of a less hierarchical and more reciprocal approach to research, teaching, learning, and outreach.

These principles led ESLARP to offer residents a determining role in project selection and planning and to involve residents, as co-investigators at each step in the planning process. ESLARP shared project-generated income with our community partners and created a community-controlled project board to sustain local development efforts beyond the university's initial commitment. ESLARP also committed itself to what Myles Horton called "the long haul" by giving the partnership the time it required to get to scale in order to address the structural causes of inequality within the city and region.

These values, which Philip Selznick referred to in *Leadership and Administration* as institutional commitments, prompted ESLARP to pursue a partnership model that was quite different from those being used on other campuses in the 1990s. In light of the Ceola Accords, ESLARP focused on resident-led change initiatives; highly participatory planning and design methods; supporting grassroots organizing that challenged the city's political machine; actions to overcome the cynicism residents felt towards planning and university research; and long-term neighborhood capacity-building and community change pursued through a highly reflective approach to research, teaching, and outreach as discussed by Don Schon.

ADAPT THE PARTNERSHIP MODEL TO THE CONTEXT

Our initial response to critiques of university-sponsored research in East St. Louis led us to embrace a participatory action research approach to community-based research as described by Lewin,

Argryis, Fals-Borda, Park, Whyte, Greenwood/Levin and others. During our initial planning efforts, we sought to involve long-time residents and leaders, on an equal basis with university-trained researchers and planners, at each step of the planning process. This "bottom-up, bottom-sideways" approach enabled us to produce an Emerson Park plan that local stakeholders believed captured their community's many assets while providing workable solutions to the major causes of disinvestment and out-migration in this historic neighborhood. While our participatory action research helped us produce a plan that was strongly supported by neighborhood residents, positively reviewed by area planners, and nationally-recognized by the American Institute of Certified Planners, these techniques did not help ESLARP build the broad base of support required to overcome the East St. Louis and St. Clair County Democratic Organization's stranglehold over local policy-making.

Participatory action research was effective in eliciting the views and mobilizing the resources of existing organizations and networks, but it was not particularly useful in expanding the membership base, leadership cadre, and skill sets of citizen organizations representing the city's poor and working-class communities. Urban places where civil society has been weakened by the structural and global forces Putnam described require an approach that could either generate or regenerate broad-based citizen organizations that could be effectively mobilized to pressure local elites to redistribute funds and services to these communities.

When ESLARP's methods proved ineffective in helping Emerson Park's leaders overcome the power inequalities that prevented the implementation of their plan, these leaders, along with the ESLARP faculty, integrated the key principles and methods of direct action organizing into their community planning approach. Following this decision, ESLARP planners and designers were no longer satisfied with the production of plans supported by existing networks of community residents; they were now committed to using their outreach, facilitation, and training resources to create broad-based citizen organizations whose leaders were prepared and skilled at disrupting the routines of local institutions to challenge their leaders to support resident-conceived and supported redevelopment plans.

This decision to integrate participatory planning with direct action organizing also resulted in a rebranding of ESLARP's community planning model. ESLARP planners no longer referred to their East St. Louis efforts, as examples of Davidoff's advocacy planning or Krumholz's equity planning—both of which privilege the role of professional planners, working either outside or inside of local government, who advocate the interests of marginalized groups. Instead, faculty began to refer to our work as an empowerment-based approach to community planning that privileged the role of citizen planners and community planning organizations, assisted by what Patrick Geddes described as "university militants" speaking and acting for themselves.

Beginning in 1991, ESLARP faculty embraced empowerment planning to influence the investment decisions of public and private institutions that determine, to a large extent, the quality of urban life by seeking to enhance the organizing, planning/design, and development capacity of community-based organizations representing the poor. We did so through an approach to community change that integrated the core theories and techniques of participatory action research and direct action organizing. While ESLARP's modified approach to community planning produced significant new investment in East St. Louis older residential neighborhoods by the mid-1990s, residents subsequently criticized our efforts for its continued privileging of the university and its students in local planning and design projects. In 1997, local residents challenged ESLARP to further modify their community-planning model by significantly increasing the residents' voice within the project.

In 1998, ESLARP faculty responded to residents' concerns regarding voice by integrating the popular education theories and methods of Paulo Freire and Myles Horton into its empowerment model of community planning. This was achieved in large part through the East St. Louis Neighborhood College that offered a dozen courses on topics selected by local residents and team -taught by a community leader and a university faculty member. These classes were designed to equip those currently organizing for change within East St. Louis' neighborhoods with theories, methods, and techniques they could use to advance "bottom-up, bottom-sideways" change efforts.

ESLARP's empowerment approach to community planning and change that integrated the key concepts and methods of participatory action research, direct action organizing, and popular education became increasingly accepted in East St. Louis in the late 1990s. Its success led to its adoption in a number of other economically distressed communities in the US and abroad including Rochester, New York; New Brunswick, New Jersey; Memphis, Tennessee; New Orleans, Louisiana; Catania, Sicily; and Sheffield, England.

Prof. Reardon addresses leaders of the Simeto River Agreement Movement in Sicily who have embraced ESLARP's "bottom-up, bottom-sideways" approach to planning and design. (Photo by Laura Saija).

While excited by the successful use of empowerment planning methods in these communities, ESLARP faculty do not believe that it is the optimal approach to use in all planning contexts. They believe it is best applied by planners and designers operating in the most challenging professional contexts, namely, those characterized by extreme economic scarcity, highly concentrated political power (machine or oligarchical rule), and considerable social distance, as measured by race, class, gender, religion and region of origin differences between the majority of community stakeholders demanding change and the professional planners and designers assisting them. In such daunting planning contexts, empowerment planning appears to be a highly effective approach to community planning for change.

USE MULTIDISCIPLINARY APPROACHES

Prior to ESLARP's inception, professional education in architecture, landscape architecture, and urban planning at UIUC was largely pursued in a "siloed" fashion. With the exception of Introduction to City and Regional Planning, a required course for undergraduate architecture, civil engineering, geography, landscape architecture, and urban planning majors, students in these design-oriented disciplines were not required to take interdisciplinary lectures, seminars or studios during their undergraduate and/or graduate education. As a result, most students in these programs knew very little about the historical origins, unique roles and contributions, key theories and concepts, technical language, and basic methods used by those outside of their own narrowly bounded discipline. While architects, landscape architects, civil engineers, and city planners were increasingly expected to work together in the "real world" to implement inspired design solutions to critical urban problems, most professional programs including those at UIUC, offered them few opportunities to work together let alone learn from each other.

When the College of Fine and Applied Arts established its Urban Extension and Minority Access Program (UEMAP) in 1987 they implemented this effort as three separate and siloed initiatives, in architecture, landscape architecture, and urban planning. When these disciplinary-based efforts failed to generate a critical mass of student, faculty, and community support after three years, a small group of faculty along with the leadership of the architecture, landscape architecture, and urban planning programs, reorganized the project as an inter-disciplinary effort.

Between 1990 and 2000, more than a dozen architecture, landscape architecture, and urban planning faculty along with hundreds of their students worked together to devise research designs, collect and analyze data, produce plans, craft architectural and urban designs, and implement neighborhood improvement projects in a manner in which it was nearly impossible to tell who was a planner versus a designer. Through ESLARP's multi-disciplinary work in East St. Louis, students and faculty, many of whom had spent years pursuing professional degrees in institutions comprised of a variety of design students without ever taking a single class with them, became intimately familiar with the history, theories, concepts, vocabularies, methods, and techniques of their fellow design professionals. During the process, the often-petty competition that exists among these professions in so many schools was replaced with a growing appreciation of the unique contributions each of these professions can make to inspire community building and place-making.

The challenging nature of the planning and design problems confronting East St. Louis and the multi-disciplinary nature of the lectures, seminars, and studios organized by ESLARP made the College's East St. Louis-related course offerings among the most popular in the College of Fine and Applied Arts. During ESLARP's first ten years of existence, it was common for many of the very best architecture, landscape architecture, and urban planning graduate students to select ESLARP studios for two or three of their required studios and to select an East St. Louis-related topic for their thesis and/or capstone projects. Within ESLARP, faculty joked that these East St. Louis-focused students should be awarded dual degrees, their primary professional degree in architecture, landscape architecture, and urban planning, as well as a second "area studies" diploma in East St. Louis Studies.

The opportunity to participate in a multi-disciplinary urban transformation project in East St. Louis became increasingly important for student recruitment. The opportunity to develop one's professional knowledge and skills in the context of a challenging experiential learning program involving a growing number of disciplines also made faculty positions in the College of Fine and Applied Arts more attractive. ESLARP gave the heads of the departments of Landscape Architecture and Urban and Regional Planning and the director of the School of Architecture responsible for the recruitment of faculty in an increasingly competitive employment market something significant to talk about when a reluctant candidate cited the campus's rural and centrally isolated location a concern.

I had studied and taught in Cornell University's College of Architecture, Art, and Planning where the presence of three internationally recognized design programs had been long heralded, but where students rarely had the opportunity to study, conduct research, prepare plans, and create and execute building/urban designs together.

I quickly came to appreciate UIUC's multi-disciplinary approach to professional education, made possible through the collaborative planning and design work taking place in East St. Louis. By the mid-1990s, the ESLARP had become one of the most distinctive and celebrated aspects of professional education within UIUC's College of Fine and Applied Arts.

AVOID COOKIE-CUTTERS

As campus and community interest in ESLARP grew during the latter half of the 1990s, several elected officials from other cities in Illinois asked UIUC's to expand the project to their municipality. Among these communities were Springfield, Peoria, Cairo, and UIUC's home community of Champaign-Urbana. Chiding UIUC's Vice-President for Public Service for focusing so much attention on East St. Louis at the expense of its "home" community, a religious leader from Champaign asked, "Your faculty had to travel one hundred and eighty miles to find poor African-Americans to work with when all they had to do was walked across University Avenue in Champaign?"

While ESLARP's faculty was pleased by the growing interest in the project among those seeking to stabilize severely distressed neighborhoods within their own communities, we did not believe that our model of community planning could simply be exported in a cookie-cutter fashion to other parts of the state. While making ourselves available to share our East St. Louis experiences with cooperative extension staff, university faculty, and campus administrators exploring how to support grassroots change and municipal reform efforts in these communities, we did not succumb to the "McDonald's franchise" urge to see the project replicated in every Illinois and midwestern city experiencing economic distress. Keenly aware of the time and effort required to establish sufficient trust among community partners to create, over time, a "context appropriate" model for community transformation, we encouraged UIUC administrators to identify faculty from other academic units on campus to initiate work in these communities.

15. REFLECTING ON THE ROAD LESS TRAVELLED

IF YOU HAD TOLD ME IN 1990 that my students and I would spend a decade working together in East St. Louis I would have told you that you were crazy. However, that is exactly what happened. What I expected to be a one-year involvement in studio projects became something much more than this.

The invitation from Rep. Younge and Ceola Davis to establish an ongoing partnership with EPDC and its sister community development organization offered my students, my colleagues, and myself an extraordinary opportunity to cross what Ira Katznelson described as the pervasive system of "city trenches" that often makes cooperation across the racial, class, ethnic, religious, gender, age, and region of origins differences that separate people so difficult in our society.

Through periods of intense fieldwork, my students and I came to a deeper appreciation of the structural causes of uneven patterns of metropolitan development affecting older industrial cities such as East St. Louis. We also came to better understand the extraordinary effort, intelligence, and creativity East St. Louis residents applied on a daily basis to protecting their homes, local institutions, and neighborhoods as safe and nurturing places to raise and enjoy their families.

The decades-long commitment to improving the quality of life in East St. Louis' neighborhoods undertaken by local leaders such as Davis and her neighbors inspired ESLARP students and faculty to do our best work. When this work produced concrete improvements in the lives of the city's most vulnerable families this had a profound effect on all those participating in the project.

The students and faculty most intimately involved in the planning and management of ESLARP's major improvement projects came to appreciate the important contribution their knowledge and skills could make to advancing resident-led change efforts in severely distressed communities. They also came to understand the significant contribution local residents' knowledge and skills could make towards improving their research, planning, and design practice. These insights into the reciprocal nature of research, planning, and design within community-university partnerships such as ESLARP was initially experienced as threatening to some ESLARP participants who strongly embraced what Whyte described as the professional-expert model of practice. The experience of seeing resident leaders offer pithy observations, unique insights, and innovative solutions to challenges ESLARP faced helped these participants move towards a deep and profound commitment to cooperative inquiry and action.

The opportunity to facilitate and manage a series of projects that brought together highly diverse groups of people to explore, analyze, and take action to address serious urban problems facing a historic African-American community like East St. Louis was life changing for me! To see some of the most and least privileged segments of our society working together, to understand and solve serious problems, and in the process, be challenged to reevaluate their own privilege, the role of a land grant institution, and their professional responsibility to produce policies, plans, and designs that advance social equity and democracy was both exhilarating and exhausting!

To observe the quality of the plans and designs generated by ESLARP students, and the commitment these students made to support residents' efforts to implement these projects in the highly-contested political terrain of East St. Louis, was profoundly moving for me as a young faculty member. The pride I experienced watching our students working shoulder to shoulder with East St. Louis activists has only been eclipsed, in recent years, by the joy I have felt observing the impressive work so many former ESLARP students have pursued to advance equity promoting strategies for other underserved communities, based upon their East St. Louis experiences.

Offering the gift of hope to those struggling to address serious urban problems was identified by long-time Portland State planning scholar, Paul Neibanck, as the most important contribution planners can make to society. By working with East St. Louis's most inspired grassroots leaders to, in the words of Cleveland's long-time planning director, Norm Krumholz, "expand opportunities for those with the fewest choices," my ESLARP faculty colleagues and I were deeply fortunate. For a decade we had the opportunity to: assist our students in pursuing public work that helped many of them discover lives of commitment and meaning; UIUC, to define an urban service mission worthy of its land grant status, and faculty from other campuses to imagine and create more transformative community/ university partnerships – an undeserved blessing for which we are all deeply grateful.

AFTERWORD

THEN WHAT HAPPENED?

Shortly after ESLARP's 10th Anniversary in 1997, Brian Orland and I, accepted positions at other universities. Under Mike Andrejasich's leadership, ESLARP continued to attract talented students and faculty committed to advancing resident-led revitalization in East St. Louis' poorest communities. This work was sustained and expanded through the efforts of a new generation of UIUC faculty, including Lynn Dearborn, Stacy Harwood, and Janni Sorensen. In 2007 UIUC transferred responsibility for its engaged scholarship portfolio in East St. Louis to its sister institution—Southern University of Illinois at Edwardsville whose students and faculty continue to provide community planning and design assistance to East St. Louis residents, organizations, and agencies. This work is carried out through the East St. Louis Action Network located in the Institute for Urban Research directed by Dr. Howard Rambsy.

While conditions in many of the neighborhoods where ESLARP focused its planning and design efforts, especially Emerson Park and Winstanley/Industry Park, show clear signs of improvement, East St. Louis continues to experience significant disinvestment, out-migration, fiscal distress, and municipal corruption. Meanwhile, a new generation of local residents, business owners, and institutional leaders inspired, in part, by the accomplishments of ESLARP supported community development corporations, are aggressively pursuing new educational improvement, economic development, affordable housing and municipal reform policies and programs aimed at reversing the city's decades of decline. These efforts currently face formidable funding challenges given the severity of Illinois' fiscal problems and the neoliberal policies of the Trump administration.

In spite of these obstacles, East St. Louis' current civic leaders have successfully undertaken significant community development projects. Among the most impressive of these are the:

- Re-opening of the Katherine Dunham Center for Art and Humanity;
- Successful development of Jazz Place as a thriving senior housing community located at Emerson Park's 15th Street MetroLink Station;
- Construction of 40 apartments

for seniors, 160 units of single-family housing, and 10 rehabilitated units by Mt. Sinai Missionary Baptist in the heart of the Winstanley/Industry Park neighborhood

- Launch of "I Am East St. Louis," a dynamic web-based arts, culture, and news network serving the city and the Metro East region
- Opening of the second phase of the Parsons Place Project, as a mixed-use, mixed-finance development by McCormack, Baron, Salazar Associates in Emerson Park
- Expansion of Emerson Park's YouthBuild Construction Trades Training to include ex-offenders returning to the community

Sinai Village Phase I in the Winstanley/Industry Park neighborhood

Jazz Center at Emerson Park's 15th Street MetroLink Station, Photo by K. Reardon, 2018

WHERE ARE THEY NOW?

ESLARP's Former Students

Several of ESLARP's dedicated graduate research assistants choose to continue their work in East St. Louis following their graduation from the U of I. Vickie Forby Kimmel has served as the Executive Director of the Emerson Park Development Corporation for the past twenty years developing an impressive set of educational and job training programs for at-risk youth. Don Johnson founded Community Development Associates, a for-profit design/build firm that has constructed more than 200 quality homes in East St. Louis and its surrounding communities.

Other former ESLARP graduate students have applied what they learned working for change in East

St. Louis to advance transformative change in other cities. After working as a community organizer for the Resurrection Project in Chicago's Pilsen neighborhood, Juan Salgado founded the Instituto Del Progreso Latino, received a MacArthur Foundation Innovation Prize and was appointed the Chancellor of the City of Chicago Community Colleges. After serving as a Community Planner in Prince George's County, MD, Michelle Whetten joined the staff of the Enterprise Community Partners where she currently serves as a Vice-President and Gulf Coast Market Leader managing a $220 million housing and community development portfolio. After directing the Rochester and New York City Offices of the Enterprise Community Partners, Rafael Cestero was appointed Commissioner of New York City's Department of Housing Preservation and Development before becoming the President and CEO of the Community Preservation Corporation. Following his service as WIPNO's first Executive Director, Kirk Goodrich, became an Economic Development Specialist with the Philadelphia Redevelopment Authority before becoming a special needs housing developer for the Enterprise Community Partners and the Monadnock Development Corporation. Following his work as NTAC's Executive Director, Damon Y. Smith enrolled in Harvard Law School where he followed Barack Obama as the second African American editor of the Harvard Law Review, taught community development law at Rutgers University—Camden before serving as Chief Counsel for HUD Secretary Sean Donovan during the Obama administration. Janni Sorensen completed her Ph.D. in Urban and Regional Planning at UIUC following her work on the second Emerson Park Improvement Plan, became a tenured professor at the University of North Carolina at Charlotte where she founded the Charlotte Action Research Project, which is modeled after ESLARP.

ESLARP's Former Faculty

Mike Andrejasich retired from the UIUC faculty in 2016 after coordinating ESLARP for nearly twenty years and serving as Acting Dean of the School of Architecture for seven years. Brian Orland served as a Professor, Head of the Department of Landscape Architecture, and Director of the Stuckeman School of Architecture and Landscape Architecture at Penn State University before being appointed the Rado Family Foundation/UGAF Professor of Geodesign, a named chair in the College of Environment and Design at the University of Georgia. After leaving UIUC, I served as a tenured faculty member and chair of the graduate planning programs at

Photo of Rafael Cestero, Kirk Goodrich, Karna Gerich, and Juan Salgado, Photo by Ken Reardon

Cornell University and the University of Memphis before accepting an appointment as a Professor and Director of the MS in Urban Planning and Community Development at the University of Massachusetts Boston in 2015.

ESLARP's Former Community Partners

State Representative Wyvetter H. Younge passed away in 2008 after representing East St. Louis and the Metro East Region for more than three decades. Ceola Davis retired as a Community Outreach Worker for the Lessie Bates Davis Neighborhood House in the early 2000s. Before her passing in 2013, she received the Lifetime Achievement Award from the East-West Gateway Coordinating Council and the Dale Prize for Excellence in Community Planning from California Polytechnic University in Pomona. Richard Suttle served as the President of the Emerson Park Development Corporation for many years before his passing in 2012. Rev. Herman L. Watson continues to serve as the Pastor of Mt. Sinai Missionary Baptist Church, which continues to develop innovative youth development programs and affordable housing services for East St. Louis through its own community development corporation. Rev. Gary Wilson retired as Pastor of the Wesley Bethel United Methodist, which he led for more than thirty years. Bill Kreeb retired as Executive Director of the Lessie Bates Davis Neighborhood House in 2016 after serving the Greater East St. Louis community for thirty-six years.

Former East St. Louis Officials

Carl Office Jr. who first served as East St. Louis' mayor from 1979 to 1991, when ESLARP was launched, continues to co-manage his family's funeral business. Following his departure from office, Office earned a divinity degree before returning for a second tenure as mayor beginning in 2003 and ending in 2007. Following his second mayoralty term, he served on East St. Louis School District 189's board. Gordon Bush, who served as East St. Louis' mayor during ESLARP's most active period, currently serves as St. Clair County Assessor and is a faculty member at Southern University of Illinois at Edwardsville where he teaches public administration. Ishaq Shafiq, my former graduate research assistant, who went on to become East St. Louis' City Manager during the Bush Administration, is currently the President of Alexandria Theology School and Managing Partner of Quantum III Consultants Group LLC which provides human resources and diversity training for public, private, and non-profit organizations.

ACKNOWLEDGEMENTS

THIS BOOK DESCRIBES the origins, evolution, accomplishments, and failures of a long-term community development partnership involving neighborhood residents, business owners, institutional leaders, and municipal officials from East St. Louis, Illinois and students, staff, and faculty from the University of Illinois at Urbana-Champaign (UIUC). This partnership came into existence through the vision of the late State Representative Wyvetter H. Younge (D-East St. Louis) who challenged UIUC, as Illinois' land grant university, to reaffirm its commitment to public scholarship, and to Dr. Stanley O. Ikenberry, former President of the University of Illinois and the American Council on Education, whose positive response to this request led to the creation of the Urban Extension and Minority Assistance Project in the fall of 1987.

The majority of the most difficult community-building activities described in this book were carried out by civic leaders representing East St. Louis' neighborhood associations, faith-based organizations, social service agencies, minority businesses, and municipal agencies who were organized by Ceola Davis, a long-time community activist

employed by the Lessie Bates Davis Neighborhood House, and a small group of deeply committed women from the Emerson Park neighborhood.

The unique community/university development partnership could not have been launched and sustained for more than a quarter of a century without strong support from numerous UIUC administrators, including: Presidents Stanley Ikenberry and James Stukel, Chancellor Michael Aiken, Deans of the College of Fine and Applied Arts Kathryn Martin and Kathleen Conlin, Director of the School of Architecture R. Alan Forester, Head of the Department of Landscape Architecture Vincent A. Bellafiore, and Head of the Department of Urban and Regional Planning Lewis D. Hopkins.

During UEMP's early years, dozens of UIUC faculty from every professorial rank and a wide range of academic units came together to undertake a dizzying array of research projects in response to critical issues identified by local residents. Among the faculty who made significant contributions to the project's early success were: Vincent Bellafiore, Ernie Clay, Kieran Donaghy, Carolyn Dry,

Carol Emmerling-DiNovo, Cynthia Geerdes, Len Heumann, Kevin Hinders, Lew Hopkins, Earl Jones, Gary Kessler, Sheldon Landsberger, Roland Liebert, Cary McDonald, Patsie Petrie, Jeff Poss, Joyce Ann Pressley, Varkki George Pallathucheril, Bob Selby, Janni Sorensen, Nina Tarr, and Bruce Wicks.

Recruiting and coordinating the efforts of this talented group of faculty with me were Professors Mike Andrejasich (Architecture), Brian Orland (Landscape Architecture). Over the course of hundreds of meetings, classes, hearings, field research days and so-called "work weekends" in East St. Louis, I had the good fortune of learning from these two outstanding scholars whose work reflected equal parts of C. Wright Mills' sociological imagination, Jack Mezirow's transformative education, Thich Nhat Hahn's engaged Buddhism, and Groucho Marx's sardonic wit.

During its first decade of operation, UIUC's East St. Louis project attracted and benefitted from the work of an impressive group of deeply committed graduate research assistants. Among these individuals were Ishaq Shafiq who became the special assistant to Mayor Gordon Bush and subsequently East St. Louis' City Manager; Don Johnson who established Community Development Associates (the city's only design/build architectural firm); Damon Y.

Smith who served as the founding director of UIUC's East St. Louis Neighborhood Technical Assistance Center; Kirk A. Goodrich who became the founding director of the Winstanley/Industry Park Development Organization; LaTonya Burton Webb who became a planner for the City of East St. Louis; and Vickie Forby who became and remains the executive director of the Emerson Park Development Corporation and Principal of its Youthbuild Academy Charter School.

Supporting our students and faculty during their early East St. Louis fieldwork activities was a talented administrative team that worked tirelessly to ensure the project had the financial resources, administrative back up, and logistical support to be effective. Among this group were Gracie Baker, Kay McBroom, Kathy Sarnecki, Glenda Fisher and Jane Terry. As the project grew with the support of external funding, it was fortunate to hire gifted staff members, including: Vickie Eddings, Dan Hoffman, James Jones, Craig Miller, Tom Shields, Damon Smith, Deanna Koenigs, and LaTonya Burton Webb.

I have done my best to reconstruct the thrills, spills, and chills of ESLARP's early years in the belief that an unvarnished history of this highly regarded and often referenced community/university development partnership will be of value to those currently seeking to mobilize

ESLARP's founding faculty members, Professors Reardon, Andrejasich, and Orland at the "build out weekend" for the Illinois Avenue Playground (Photo by ESLARP Staff)

campus resources to advance resident-led change in other distressed communities. I take full responsibility for any errors and/or omissions made in preparing this manuscript and strongly encourage former ESLARP participants and observers to inform me of these mistakes so they may be corrected.

I also want to thank my former students and colleagues at the University of Illinois at Urbana-Champaign, Cornell University, The University of Memphis, and The University of Massachusetts Boston as well as those at the Association of Collegiate Schools of Planning, American Planning Association, Urban Affairs Association, Campus Compact, and Planners Network for encouraging me to complete this book. I am especially grateful for the financial support and leaves the University of Illinois at Urbana-Champaign, Cornell University, and The University of Memphis provided to support this project.

I also want to thank Maya Reardon for selecting and modifying the photographs that appear in this book which represent an important contribution to the telling of this remarkable resurrection story. Finally, I want to express my deep gratitude to Mary Rowles and Wade Rathke of Social Policy Press for their skillful editing of this story.

REFERENCES

Adams, Frank and Myles Horton. 1975. *Unearthing the Seeds of Highlander.* Winston-Salem, NC: John F. Blair Publishing.

Alinsky, Saul D. 1946. *Reveille for Radicals.* New York: Random House.

Angotti, Tom. 2011. *New York for Sale: Community Planning Confronts Global Real Estate.* Cambridge, MA: MIT Press.

Argyris, Chris, Robert N. Putnam, and Diana McLain Smith. 1985. *Action Science: Concepts, Methods, and Skills for Research and Intervention.* San Francisco, CA: Jossey-Bass Publishing Inc.

Argyris, Chris and Donald A. Schon. 1978. *Organizational Learning: A Theory of Action Perspective.* Reading, MA: Addison-Wesley Publishing Company.

Arnstein, Sherry R. 1984. "Ladder of Citizen Participation." *Journal of the American Institute of Certified Planners,* Vol. 35, No. 4, July 1969.

Aschenbrenner, Joyce. 2002. *Katherine Dunham: Dancing a Life.* Urbana, IL: University of Illinois Press.

Adanri, Bayo et. al. 1991. *Emerson Park Neighborhood Improvement Plan.* Champaign-Urbana: Department of Urban and Regional Planning.

Bartholomew, Harland. 1926. *Plan for East St. Louis Illinois.* East St. Louis, Illinois: City Planning Commission.

Bobo, Kim, Jackie Kendall, and Steve Max. 2001. *Organize! Organizing for Social Change: The Midwest Academy Manual for Activists.* Santa Anna, CA: Seven Locks Press.

Boyer. Ernest L. 1994. "Creating the New American College." *The Chronicle of Higher Education,* March 9, 1994, XL (27), A48.

Bratton, William J. and George L. Kelling. 2015. "Why We Need Broken Windows Policing." *City Journal,* Winter.

Cestero, Rafael, Karna Gerich, Kirk Goodrich and Juan Salgado. 1993. *Winstanley/Industry Park Neighborhood: Five-Year Neighborhood Demonstration Area Strategic Community Stabilization Plan.* Urbana: Department of Urban and Regional Planning.

Chapin Jr., F. Stuart and Edward J. Kaiser. 1979. *Urban Land Use Planning, Third Edition*. Urbana, IL: University of Illinois Press.

Chen, Elizabeth. 2014. *Recovering an Anthropological Legacy: Choreographing Ethnographic Futures*. Sante Fe, NM: School of Advanced Research Process.

Cisneros, Henry G. 1996. *The University and the Urban Challenge*. Washington, DC: U.S. Department of Housing and Urban Development.

Clavel, Pierre. 1986. *The Progressive City: Planning and Participation 1969-1984*. New Brunswick, NJ: Rutgers University Press.

Coughlin, David and Mary Brydon-Miller. 2014. *The SAGE Encyclopedia of Action Research*, Thousand Oaks, CA: Sage Publications Inc.

Crowe, Timothy D. 1991. *Crime Prevention Through Environmental Design: Application of Architectural Design and Space Management Concepts*. Louisville, KY: National Crime Prevention Institute.

Davidoff, Paul. 1965. "Advocacy Planning and Pluralism in Planning." *J ournal of the American Institute of Planners*, 31(4).

DePriest, Maria et. al. 1992. *The Winstanley/Industry Park Neighborhood Improvement Plan*. Urbana: Department of Urban and Regional Planning.

Dubois, Rene. 1971. *"Trend is Not Destiny."* Engineering and Science, 34(3).

Fals-Borda, Orlando and Mohammad Rahman. 1991. *Action and Knowledge: Breaking the Monopoly with Participatory Action Research*. New York: Roman and Littlefield Publishers.

Forester, John F. 2001. *The Deliberative Practitioner: Encouraging Participatory Planning Processes*. Cambridge, MA: MIT Press.

Paulo Friere. 1984. *Education for Critical Consciousness*. New York, NY: Bloomberg Academic.

Frost, Robert. 1920. *Mountain Interval*. New York: New York: Holt and Company.

Fuller, R. Buckminster and Kiyoshi R. Kuromiya. 1981. *Critical Path*. New York, NY: St. Martin's Press.

Gecan. Michael. 2002. *Going Public: An Organizer's Guide to Citizen Action*. New York, NY: Anchor Books.

Geddes. Patrick J. 1915. *Cities in Evolution: An Introduction to the Town Planning Movement and to the Study of Civics*. London, UK: Williams and Norgate.

Geertz, Clifford. 1983. *Local Knowledge and Further Essays in Interpretive Anthropology.* New York, NY.

Goldsmith, William W. 1998. "Fishing Bodies Out of the River: Can Universities Help Troubled Neighborhoods." *Connecticut Law Review,* Volume 30, Summer, Number 4.

Gramsci, Antonio. 1971. *Selections from the Prison Notebooks.* New York, NY: International Publishers.

Greenwood, Davydd and Morten Levin. 2007. *Introduction to Action Research, Second Edition.* Thousand Oaks, CA: Sage Publications Inc.

Gregory. Kathryn. 1997. *Strategic Plan for Eagles' Nest Transitional Housing for Wounded Veterans.* Urbana, IL: School of Architecture.

Gross, Bertram A. and Stanley Moses, "Building a Movement: Full Employment Planning from the Bottom Up." *The Nation,* April 10, 1982.

Hahn, Thich Nhat. 1975. *The Miracle of Mindfulness: An Introduction to the Practice of Meditation.* Boston, MA: Beacon Press.

Hanson, Glen. 2002. *Therapeutic Community: National Institute on Drug Abuse Research Report Series.* Washington, DC: National Institute on Drug Abuse.

Harvard Business School. 2005. *SWOT Analysis I: Looking Outside for Threats and Opportunities,* Cambridge, MA: HBS Press.

Horton, Myles. 1997. *The Long Haul: An Autobiography.* New York, NY: Columbia University Teachers' Press.

Horton, Myles and Dale Jacobs, 2003. *The Myles Horton Reader: Education for Social Change.* Knoxville, TN: University of Tennessee Press.

Horwitt, Sanford D. 1989. *Let Them Call Me Rebel: Saul Alinsky, His Life and Legacy.* New York, NY: Alfred A. Knopf.

Humphrey, Albert. 2005. "SWOT Analysis for Management Consulting," *SRI Alumni Newsletter,* December.

5 (ILCS 120/) Open Meetings Act.

Illinois Legal Aid. *Contract for Deed Home Buyers' Rights and Responsibilities.* www.illinoislegalaid.org/index.cfm?fuseaction=home.dsp_content&content ID=352, September 2011.

Kamenski, Michael D. and Sheldon Landsberger. 2000. "Heavy Metals in Urban Sectors of East St. Louis, Part I: Total Concentrations of Heavy Metals in Soils." *Journal of Air and Waste Management Association.* Volume 5, Issue 9.

Kamenski, Michael D. and Sheldon Landsberger. 2000. "Heavy Metals in Urban Soils of East St. Louis, Part II: Leaching Characteristics and Modeling." *Journal of Air and Waste Management Association*, Volume 50, Issue 9.

Kelling, George L. and James Q. Wilson. 1982. "Broken Windows: The Police and Neighborhood Safety." *The Atlantic Magazine.* March 1, 1982.

Khadamian, Ann. 2003. *Working with Culture: The Way the Job Gets Done in Public Programs.* Washington, DC: CQ Press.

King, Mel. 1999. *Chain of Change: The Struggle for Black Community Development.* Boston, MA: South End Press.

Kolb, David. 1984. *Experiential Learning: Experience as the Source of Learning and Development.* Englewood Cliffs. NJ: Prentice-Hall, Inc.

Kozol, Jonathan. 1991. *Savage Inequalities: Children in America's Schools.* New York: Random House.

Kretzmann, John P. and John L. McKnight. 1993. *Community Building from the Inside Out: A Path Toward Finding and Mobilizing a Community's Assets.* Chicago, IL: ACTA Publications.

Krumholz, Norm and John Forester. 1990. *Making Equity Planning Work: Leadership in the Public Sector.* Philadelphia, PA: Temple University Press.

Lewin, Kurt. 1948. *Resolving Social Conflicts and Field Theory in Social Science.* New York, NY: Harper and Row Inc.

Logan, John R. and Molotch, Harvey Luskin. 1987. *Urban Fortunes: The Political Economy of Place.* Berkeley, CA: University of California Press.

Lynch, Kevin. 1960. *The Image of the City.* Cambridge, MA: MIT Press.

Marx, Groucho. 1995. *Groucho and Me.* New York: First da Capo Press.

Medoff, Peter and Holly Sklar. 1994. *Holding Ground: The Fall and Rise of An Urban Neighborhood.* Boston, MA: South End Press.

Mezirow, Jack. 1989. "Transformative Theory and Social Action: A Response to Collard and the Law," *Adult Education Quarterly*, 39(3).

Mintzberg, Henry. 1994. "The Fall of Strategic Planning." *Harvard Business Review,* January-February.

Mills, C.W. 1959. *The Sociological Imagination*. London, UK: The Oxford University Press.

Naffziger, Chris. 2014. "Ghost of the Stockyards: The Last Traces of National City," *St. Louis Magazine*, September 24, 2014, www.stlmag.com/arts/history/ghosts-of-the-stockyards/

New Solutions Group, LLC (nsgdetroit.com). 2013. *Placemaking in Legacy Cities: Opportunities and Good Practice*. Washington, DC: Center for Community Progress.

O'Connor, Barbara. 2000. *Katherine Dunham: Pioneer of Black Dance*. Minneapolis, MN: Carolrhoda Books Inc.

Park, Peter, Mary Brydon-Miller, Budd Hall, and Ted Jackson. 1993. *Voices of Change: Participatory Research in the United States and Canada*. Westport, CT: Bergin and Garvey.

Peters, Scott J. 2010. *Democracy and Higher Education: Traditions and Stories of Civic Engagement*. East Lansing, MI: Michigan State University Press.

Public Law 88-352, 78 Statute 241, July 2, 1964.

Putnam, Robert D. 1995. "Bowling Alone: America's Declining Social Capital." *Journal of Democracy*. Vol. 6, no. 1 (January 1995).

Putnam, Robert D. 2000. *Bowling Alone: The Collapse and Revival of American Community*. New York, NY: Simon and Schuster.

Reardon, Kenneth. 1999. "A Sustainable Community/University Partnership," *Liberal Education*, Volume 85, Number 3, Summer.

—2003. "Ceola's Vision, Our Blessing: The Study of an Evolving Community/University Partnership in East St. Louis." Barbara Eckstein and James A. Throckmorton (Eds.) *Story and Sustainability: Planning, Practice and Possibilities for American Cities*. Cambridge, MA: MIT Press.

—1995. "Community-Building in East St. Louis: The Illinois Avenue Playground." Washington, DC: *AICP Casebook Series*.

—2005. "Empowerment Planning in East St. Louis: A Peoples' Response to the Deindustrialization Blues." *CITIES*, Volume 9, Number 1.

—1998. "Enhancing the Capacity of Community-Based Organizations in East St. Louis." *Journal of Planning Education and Research*.

—1990. *Local Economic Development in Chicago 1983-1987: The Reform Efforts of Harold Washington*, unpublished doctoral dissertation, Cornell University: Ithaca, NY.

—1989. "Public Markets and Urban Social Life." Judith DeSena (eds.)
Contemporary Readings in Sociology, Dubuque, IA: Kendall-Hall Publishing.

Ryan, William. 1972. *Blaming the Victim.* New York, NY: Random House Inc.

Sandercock, Leonie. 2003. *Cosmopolis II: Mongrel Cities in the 21st Century.*
New York: Bloomsbury Academic. pp. 166-172.

Schon, Donald A. 1984. *The Reflective Practitioner: How Professionals Think
and Act.* New York, NY: Basic Books Inc.

Selznick, Philip. 1984. *Leadership in Administration: A Sociological
Interpretation.* Berkeley, CA: University of California Press.

Sorensen, Janni, et. al. 1997. *The Emerson Park Revitalization Plan.*
Urbana: Department of Urban and Regional Planning.

Steinbaug, Thomas G. and Jill Avery. 2010. *Marketing Analysis Toolkit:
Situational Analysis, Background Notes.* Cambridge, MA:
Harvard Business School Press.

Stephens, Richard B. 1994. *Plannerese Dictionary.* Pomona: Department
of Urban and Regional Planning, College of Environmental Design,
California State Polytechnic University at Pomona.

Stone, Clarence N. 1989. *Regime Politics: Governing Atlanta 1946-1988.*
Lawrence: University of Kansas Press.

Strober, Myra H. 2011. *Interdisciplinary Communication: Challenging Habits of
Thought.* Palo Alto: Stanford University Press.

Sullivan, Donald G. 1981. *Neighborhood Planning Workshop Syllabus.* New
York, NY: Graduate Program in Urban Affairs, City College of New York.

Thompson, E.P. 1966. *The Making of the English Working Class.* New York, NY:
Alfred A. Knopf.

Urban Extension and Minority Access Project. 1988, 1989, and 1990. *Annual
Reports of the East St. Louis Urban Extension and Minority Access Project,*
Carolyn L. Dry (eds.), Champaign, IL: College of Fine and Applies Arts,
University of Illinois at Urbana-Champaign.

Von Clausewitz, Carl. 1834. *On War,* edited by Michael Howard and Pila
Paret. Princeton, NJ: Princeton University Press.

Whyte, William F. 1984. *Learning From The Field: A Guide From Experience.*
Thousand Oaks, CA: Sage Publications Inc.

—1990. *Participatory Action Research*. Newbury Park, CA: Sage Publications Inc.

—1983. "Social Inventions for Human Problem Solving: ASA Presidential Address." *Journal of the American Sociological Association*, spring, 1983.

Wicks, Bruce E. and Cary McDonald, 1996. *Establishing a Cultural District in East St. Louis, IL: Preliminary Proposal*. Urbana, IL: Department of Leisure Studies.

Wilkerson, Isabel. 1991. "Ravaged City on Mississippi Flounders," *New York Times*, April 4, 1991

SOCIAL POLICY PUBLICATIONS

Social Policy

The journal *Social Policy* is now entering its 50th year and is published quarterly and on-line at www.socialpolicy.org.

Subscriptions are available for individuals and institutions. Inquire with publisher@socialpolicy.org for the current rates.

Social Policy Press Titles

Lessons from the Field: Organizing in Rural Communities, Joe Szakos and Kristin Layng Szakos (editors), 2008. Available $15.00 plus shipping.

The Battle for the Ninth Ward: ACORN, Rebuilding New Orleans, and the Lessons of Disaster, Wade Rathke (2011). Available $20.00 plus shipping and as an e-book.

Global Grassroots: Perspectives on International Organizing, Wade Rathke (editor), (2011). Available $20.00 plus shipping and as an e-book.

Guns and Kids: Can We Survive the Carnage, Franklin Strier, (2015). Available as an e-book.

Building Power, Changing Lives: The Story of Virginia Organizing, Ruth Berta and Amanda Leonard Pohl, (2015).Available $20.00 plus shipping.

Nuts and Bolts: The ACORN Fundamentals of Organizing, Wade Rathke (2018). Available $35.00 and as an e-book.

Campaigns: Lessons from the Field, Wade Rathke (editor), (2018). Available $15.00 and as an e-book.

Building Bridges: Community and University Partnership in East St. Louis, Kenneth Reardon, (2019). Available $20.00.

INDEX

unemployed, unemployment, 43, 80, 128-129

unions, 17

University of Illinois Urbana-Champaign (UIUC), 9, 11-17, 20-25, 27, 29, 31-32, 34, 45, 49, 51, 53, 55, 57-58, 60, 62, 65, 67, 69-70, 72, 75, 81, 84, 91, 97-98, 100-101, 104-105, 107, 110-111, 115-117, 121-126, 130-132, 134, 136, 139, 143-148, 154, 157, 159, 162-163, 165, 168-169, 171, 176, 178, 181-182, 184

University of Manitoba, 152

University of San Paulo, 144, 151

UNRISD's Voluntary Action for Local Democracy Project, 149, 151-152

Urban Extension and Minority Access Program (UEMAP), 9, 11-16, 21, 23, 25, 66, 139, 176

V

vacant, 18, 30, 43, 45, 55, 78, 82, 93, 96, 103, 127

veterans, veteran, 71, 146

violence, 18, 28, 33, 43, 83

vision, visionary, 76-78, 96, 101, 159-160

W

Watson, Rev. Herman, 68, 71, 80, 98, 100, 109-110, 118, 122, 186

Wesley Bethel United Methodist, 67, 69, 78, 80, 83, 85-86, 93, 103, 110, 186

Westendorff, David, 149, 151

Whetten, Michelle, 85, 113, 122, 184

Whyte, William Foote, 41, 139, 173, 180

Wicks, Bruce, 125-126

William, Bratton, 50

Wilson, Rev. Gary, 67-68, 71, 73-74, 80, 83, 103, 109-110, 117, 186

Winstanley Industrial Park, 67-69, 71-73, 75, 77-81, 86-87, 90-93, 95, 121, 124-126, 140, 162, 169, 182-183

Winstanley Industrial Park Neighborhood Organization (WIPNO), 67-68, 71-80, 82, 86, 88-96, 100-103, 105, 110-111, 113-115, 117-118, 120, 122-123, 184

women, 11, 18-20, 28, 32, 43, 105-106, 169

workers, workforce, 10, 17, 35, 45, 80, 107, 151, 158, 161, 186

Y

Younge, Wyvetter, 9, 11-13, 21, 34, 44, 47, 53-54, 56, 60, 62, 65, 78, 84, 102-103, 111, 115, 122, 125, 136, 142, 169, 179, 185

youth, 47, 60, 67, 85, 92, 97, 100-101, 106, 111, 127, 129, 183, 186

YouthBuild, 183